UNDERSTANDING
J. BRUCE ISMAY

Understanding
J. Bruce Ismay

The True Story of the Man They Called 'The Coward of Titanic'

Clifford Ismay

Foreword by Tad Fitch

This book is dedicated to the memory of my father Cecil Ismay, a wonderful man who showed me the stars.

Titanic sinking animation on back cover courtesy of HFX Studios, directed by Thomas Lynskey and animated by Levi Rourke. Model artwork by Liam Sharpe and Michael Brady. Animation was produced under the historical guidance of J. Kent Layton, Tad Fitch, and Bill Wormstedt.

First published 2022

The History Press
97 St George's Place, Cheltenham,
Gloucestershire, GL50 3QB
www.thehistorypress.co.uk

British Library Cataloguing in Publication Data.
A catalogue record for this book is available from the British Library.

ISBN 978 0 7509 9866 6

Typesetting and origination by The History Press
Printed and bound in Great Britain by TJ Books Limited, Padstow, Cornwall.

Trees for LYfe

CONTENTS

FOREWORD BY TAD FITCH

Bruce Ismay is among the most easily recognisable figures of the *Titanic* disaster. This is partially because he was the chairman and managing director of the White Star Line. However, he is even more recognised due to the tremendous amount of character assassination that he was subjected to in the yellow press following the sinking. This built up a subjective and largely negative caricature of the actual man, one that has unfortunately stood the test of time. Even though it makes for a dramatic story, this portrayal of J. 'Brute' Ismay, the so-called 'Coward of the *Titanic*', does not stand up to scrutiny or to a close study of the historical facts.

Besides the negative impact that the rumours and subsequent attempts at character assassination had on Ismay and his family, it also virtually erased the real Bruce, the human, from the historic record. Misconceptions and myths surround nearly every aspect of his involvement with *Titanic*, from basic information about the design and safety provisions aboard the ship, to his actions during the maiden voyage, and even extending into his later life.

Cliff Ismay has done a great service in writing this biography. Far from being a hagiography designed simply to refute popular myths about the man related to *Titanic*, here is a true, rounded portrait of his kinsman, the man Bruce Ismay truly was. No longer will we know Bruce just from his actions, both alleged and true, on 14–15 April 1912. In these pages, you will learn about the Ismay family's background and origins, and how they became involved in shipbuilding. You will learn about Bruce's father, Thomas Henry Ismay, and how their difficult relationship had a profound impact on his personality. A shy and sensitive individual, Bruce would often hide this side of himself behind a discourteous façade, as a form of compensating. Readers will also learn of his courtship and eventual marriage to his wife Julia, and about their children.

You will learn how, far from being the cold, uncaring individual portrayed in movies, Bruce was described as a charming and warm host by those who got to know him and was extremely charitable to those around him, even if he was described as sometimes being taciturn and abrupt in his business dealings. Readers will also learn how, even though Ismay was greatly impacted and traumatised by the *Titanic* disaster, he did not withdraw from society or become a recluse, contrary to popular myth. In fact, he attempted to revoke his planned retirement from the International Mercantile Marine, the parent company of the White Star Line, following the sinking. He would maintain multiple business dealings throughout the remainder of his life.

For those who are interested in learning the true history of those aboard *Titanic*, Cliff Ismay has done an invaluable service. This book will be enlightening and fascinating to many and is a welcome addition to the 'human story' of Titanic. I hope that readers will enjoy getting to know the real Bruce Ismay as much as I did.

Tad Fitch
Cleveland, Ohio

Tad Fitch is a member of the *Titanic* Historical Society and *Titanic* International Society. He has co-authored six books to date, including *Report into the Loss of SS Titanic: A Centennial Reappraisal* (2011); *On A Sea of Glass: The Life & Loss of RMS Titanic* (2012); *Titanic: Solving the Mysteries* (2019); and the forthcoming *Recreating Titanic & Her Sisters: A Visual History* (2022).

INTRODUCTION

On Sunday, 14 April 1912, RMS *Titanic*, at that time the largest moving object built by the hand of man, collided with an iceberg during her maiden voyage from Southampton to New York, resulting in the loss of more than 1,500 lives. From that moment, the actions of Joseph Bruce Ismay, chairman of *Titanic*'s operating company, the White Star Line, would be scrutinised for over a century.

In modern times, the story has become ingrained in popular culture: 'the world's largest, most luxurious ocean liner sinks to the bottom of the Atlantic Ocean without an adequate number of lifeboats for all on board'. While the tragedy still captures people's hearts and minds over a century later, no other individual within the narrative remains more controversial than Joseph Bruce Ismay.

The status of Ismay while aboard *Titanic* has been open to much discussion over recent years. It would be true to say that Bruce was chairman of the White Star Line and president of the International Mercantile Marine, although he was not on board in either capacity. According to the ship's manifest, Bruce was listed as a First Class passenger, not as an employee of the White Star Line.

At the time of the collision, Bruce was resting in his cabin and was alerted by a sudden vibration, after which he lay there for a few moments. Not realising that the ship had struck ice, his first thoughts were of the colossal ship losing a propeller blade. A short while later, he left his cabin, meeting a steward in the corridor outside his room. Bruce asked what had happened, but at that point the steward was also unaware of the unfolding horror awaiting everyone on board. Bruce immediately returned to his cabin and hurriedly put on a dressing gown and a pair of slippers, before making his way to the ship's bridge. There he met *Titanic*'s captain, Edward J. Smith, who informed him that the ship had struck ice.

Bruce asked of Smith, 'Do you think the ship is seriously damaged?'

Smith replied, 'I'm afraid she is.'

On hearing Smith's reply, Bruce made his way to the lower decks, where he chanced upon the ship's carpenter, and the severity of the damage was explained to him. In the main companionway, Bruce also met Joseph Bell, the ship's chief engineer. Bell explained that the ship was taking on water and it was possible that, given the severity of the damage, the watertight compartments might not control the flooding; he also felt the pumps might only be sufficient to keep the ship afloat for one hour, or perhaps two.

Bruce proceeded back to the ship's bridge, and, upon arrival, he heard the order being given to break out the lifeboats. The chairman of the White Star Line then made his way over to *Titanic*'s starboard-side Boat Deck, where he met a ship's officer. Bruce informed him of the urgency of the situation and promptly assisted in putting women and children into many lifeboats before boarding the last lifeboat to be successfully lowered from the starboard side.

The ensuing American inquiry into the *Titanic* disaster did not directly attach any blame to Bruce, although it was felt that his mere presence on board may have contributed to Captain Smith's decision to increase speed. The following British inquiry cleared Ismay of any blame.

Immediately following the sinking of *Titanic*, Bruce Ismay was attacked by the British and American press, who, at least in part, held Bruce responsible for the *Titanic* disaster and for the fact that he was saved while a great many others lost their lives. American newspapers, especially those owned by Randolph Hearst, labelled him as the 'Coward of the *Titanic*' and suggested that Bruce's name should be changed to J. 'Brute' Ismay, while also suggesting the company's name should be changed from White Star to Yellow Liver.

To what extent can we question the accuracy of these criticisms?

1

The Ismay Family

To understand Joseph Bruce Ismay, it may be necessary to look back in time, not only into his life but also to examine his family history. Many Ismay family members have their roots in Cumbria, or Cumberland as it was known before English county boundary changes in 1974. The Ismay family can be traced back to at least the turn of the sixteenth century, and possibly as far back as 1066, with the Norman invasion of Britain. The surname Ismay is derived from the name of an ancestor, 'the son of Ismay', with the name originally being a rare girls' name in thirteenth-century France. The name managed to survive, later becoming a surname.

For the purpose of this chapter, we shall begin in the ancient parish of Uldale, Cumbria. Uldale is a small village located in an isolated area, among the fells of the northern edge of the English Lake District and overlooks the River Ellen which flows into the Solway Firth at Maryport.

Originally, a ninth-century Norse-Irish settlement existed there. The name Uldale comes from the Old Norse language '*úlf*', meaning 'wolf'. Dale-wolves once roamed the fells here in abundance.

A certain Daniel Ismay lived in the village with his wife, Ann. He was born in Bromfield, a small hamlet 10 miles to the north-west of Uldale. He had met and fallen in love with Ann Cowx, the daughter of John Cowx, a prominent Uldale family. Daniel and Ann, already heavily pregnant with her first child, were married in St James' Church, Uldale, on 12 November 1754, with their first son Thomas being born two months later.

In the eighteenth century, Uldale was a small village with a population of around 350 inhabitants. Villagers were mainly employed in farming, copper mining and quarrying for limestone. Daniel plied his trade as carpenter in and around Uldale for a great many years, during which time Ann gave birth to seven sons and five daughters. The last four born were all boys, but sadly, none of these four boys lived past their fifth birthday.

Thomas was the eldest of the seven brothers and attended the local grammar school, which was located close to his home to the south-east of Uldale village. As a young boy, his passion was carving pieces of wood which he would find lying around in his father's workshop. Mostly he carved small boats, inspired by pictures he found in his favourite books, and he became very good at it.

At that time, farming was the main business of the Ismay family. However, like his father, Thomas' profession was a carpenter, working alongside his father for several years. In July 1777, Thomas married Elizabeth Scott, soon after her birthday, both being 22 years of age. Soon after their marriage, Thomas and Elizabeth, who was heavily pregnant with their first child, decided to seek a new way of life and relocated to the seaside town of Maryport, Cumbria, an upcoming town which was 18 miles to the west of Uldale and situated on the shores of the Solway Firth. It was here that their first child, Henry, was born.

After several years plying his trade as a carpenter in Maryport, Thomas was enlisted as a soldier with the British Army, becoming involved with the British invasion of Guadeloupe. Thomas was subsequently captured by the French and remained a prisoner in Guadeloupe until his death in 1795, at just 40 years of age.

By the end of the eighteenth century, Maryport had a population of just under 4,000 inhabitants. The main income in the town was from importing timber from America and exporting coal to Ireland. There were three main shipbuilding yards situated on the town's River Ellen, which, being a narrow river, necessitated most ships to be launched broadside. Therefore, ships built in Maryport were typically between 30 and 450 tons, of timber construction and mainly designed for the American, Baltic and West Indian trade routes.

One of Maryport's first shipbuilding yards was owned by Joseph Middleton, and one of his ships, the *Vine*, a three-masted schooner built in 1812, was built for and first mastered by Henry Ismay, the son of Thomas and Elizabeth. In January 1800, the 23-year-old Henry married Joseph Middleton's eldest daughter, Charlotte.

Henry had been employed as Master Mariner throughout much of his adult life. His regular trading route was between Liverpool and Newfoundland, with regular stops at Queenstown in Ireland for supplies. He loved the challenging life that his profession demanded and largely remained at sea until his retirement when, along with his beloved wife, he took on a small grocery shop in Maryport's High Street, where he traded for many years as grocer and flour dealer.

Joseph Ismay, the third son of Henry and Charlotte, was christened on 27 April 1804 in the Presbyterian Church, Maryport, the town in which he would later work as a shipbuilder, ship owner and timber merchant. Following in his father's footsteps, Joseph entered into the seafaring world at an early age, finding employment as a foreman shipwright at the Middleton yard, which was now owned by his uncle, Isaac Middleton.

Joseph Ismay married Mary Sealby, daughter of John Sealby, a prominent gentleman of Maryport, immediately taking his new bride to live in the small house that he had purchased some three years earlier. This house was situated in Whillan's Yard, which was a narrow thoroughfare between two of the main streets in the town and was very close to his father's house on High Street. Being a narrow thoroughfare, all the houses were small and cramped together, and consequently, conditions in this tiny house were quite restrictive, but it made an acceptable first home for the young couple.

Four years later, their first son, Thomas Henry Ismay was born. He was destined to become one of the most prominent ship owners of his time.

2

Young Thomas Henry Ismay

T homas Henry Ismay has been described as the greatest ship-owner of the Victorian era. He was born in 1837, the year in which Queen Victoria took the throne, and died in 1899, just two years before her death. He was the first son of Joseph Ismay and was born in the family home in Whillan's Yard, Maryport, on 7 January 1837. Four years later, the family had increased to four children. Charlotte and Mary were twins, and three years later another sister, Sarah, was born.

This small three-roomed house was now overcrowded, and so they bought a larger house near the family's shipbuilding yard. Their new home was named Ropery House, so named because all the ropes connected with the shipyard were laid out nearby. The house had four main rooms and three attic rooms, thereby making an ideal home for the expanding family. It was here that their fifth child, John Ismay, was born, when Thomas was 10 years old.

Soon after moving to Ropery House, Thomas' father, Joseph, began his own business as a timber merchant and shipbuilder, he was also Maryport's first shipbroker and had a share in four ships trading with the port. One of the firms he traded with was Imrie Tomlinson, of Liverpool, with which his son Thomas would later be apprenticed.

As a young boy, Thomas spent many hours at the quayside. He loved to talk with the sailors and enjoyed watching the ships entering the port and leaving for lands afar. Although he was very young, he demonstrated his keen interest in anything to do with the sea and ships, even joining the sailors in the habit of chewing tobacco, soon becoming known as 'Baccy' Ismay.

Thomas had a happy childhood, but he had to assume a degree of responsibility at an early age. When he reached the age of 12, his father Joseph became very ill and journeyed south to Malvern, in the hope that treatment at the town's legendary and fashionable spa would aid his recovery. During his father's time away, the young Thomas helped look after his mother and his younger brother and sisters, as well as keeping the garden in good order, the produce of which would help provide a welcome meal at the family table. He also assisted with his father's business in the hope that all would be ready for his father's return.

His parents soon realised the boy's true potential, so when he left the local school, they arranged for his further education to be completed at Croft House School, Brampton, near Carlisle, almost 40 miles to the north of Maryport. This was considered, at that time, to be one of the best boarding schools in the north of England and drew pupils from all over northern England, Scotland and Ireland. The young Thomas probably travelled to school on the newly opened Maryport–Carlisle Railway, the construction of which began the year he was born. It had only been in operation since 1841 and at that time was considered by many people to be an advanced form of transportation.

The school was run by a Mr Joseph Coulthard, his wife, two sons, a daughter and four assistant masters. It comprised two large houses, standing about 200 yards apart. In one were the residential quarters and in the other, classrooms.

The curriculum taught was considered progressive for that time and mainly consisted of English, arithmetic, classics, modern languages, philosophy, deportment, penmanship, drawing and music. Philosophy included astronomy, chemistry, physiology, botany and geology, while deportment included dancing, drill and gentlemanly bearing. While he was at this school, Thomas loved nothing better than to build model boats in his spare time and rig them according to their class. Once they were complete, he would sail them on a nearby pond, much like his great grandfather Thomas had done.

An account of Thomas' days at Croft House was written by one of his contemporaries, half a century later:

Thomas Henry Ismay was, along with myself, and many others, a pupil at Croft House under the late Mr Coulthard, and survivors of that company will remember well the dark-complexioned lad, with dark piercing eyes, whose hobby was the sea, whose ambition was a seafaring life, and who never seemed so happy as when engaged in fashioning a miniature sailing vessel with a pocket knife out of a block of wood, rigging it with masts and sails all according to the orthodox rig of its class and then sailing it on the pond at Irthington. Anything affecting the sailing of ships touched him in a tender place and awakened those instincts which were destined to make his name famous throughout the world. Ismay finished his education at Croft House taking the general course of the school which was regarded as a very good course and far ahead of general notions of education in those days. I doubt whether any of his school-fellows or teachers would, in his school days, have predicted that such a future was in store for him.

After only one year at Croft House, Thomas' father died suddenly, aged only 46. It was Thomas' great-uncle, Isaac Middleton, who arranged for Thomas to be apprenticed with the shipbrokers Imrie Tomlinson, who Isaac knew well, as he and Thomas' father had conducted business. It followed that at the age of 16, Thomas began his apprenticeship at 13 Rumford Street, Liverpool. At that time, there was a regular sea route trading between Maryport and Liverpool, and it is likely that this mode of transportation was chosen for his journey.

From that moment, Thomas could be considered to be the architect of his own fortunes. His father had been successful as a shipbuilder in Maryport, but Thomas arrived in Liverpool with very little capital, yet his young mind was full of ambition and aspiration, enough to position him at the gateway to his career.

While serving his apprenticeship, Thomas had established a good relationship with Liverpool merchants, mainly because of his honesty and the prompt attention he gave to their affairs. After three years with the firm Imrie Tomlinson, Thomas decided to gain some experience of life at sea and of the world, and so embarked on a series of voyages which lasted almost a year. His first voyage was arranged with Jackson & Co. of Maryport, sailing from Liverpool to Chile on board their vessel *Charles Jackson*, a three-year-old barque of 352 tonnes. Under the command of his uncle, Captain George Metcalf, *Charles Jackson* sailed from Liverpool on 4 January 1856, destined for South America, a journey that took almost a year.

Interestingly, several years later, *Charles Jackson* came under the ownership of T.H. Ismay & Co. for a short time, before being returned to the ownership of her builders, R. Ritson & Co. During his time away, he had many adventures and thoroughly enjoyed his experience. On his return to Liverpool, in the autumn of 1856, Thomas set about putting his affairs in order.

At 20 years of age, Thomas had already become a very astute businessman and was ready to make his mark. As Thomas had only been 13 years old when his father died, his uncle Joseph Sealby was made a trustee of his father's estate. Apparently, Sealby had assigned part of the family business to his son John, particularly the management of two ships partly owned by Thomas' late father, and now by Thomas – the ships being named *Mary Ismay* and *Charles Bronwell*.

Thomas visited *Charles Bronwell* while she was moored in Liverpool and asserted to the captain of the vessel that he did not consider his cousin, John Sealby, a competent person to manage the ship. This resulted in several heated exchanges between John Sealby, Thomas Ismay and ultimately Joseph Sealby, trustee of the estate. Joseph soon decided that he no longer wished to have further business with his nephew and sold his shares to Thomas. His divisive strategy had worked, and Thomas had successfully freed himself from his trustees.

While still working for the firm Imrie Tomlinson, Thomas met a retired sea captain named Philip Nelson, who was also a son of Maryport. Nelson had an interest in anything to do with ships, and his firm was known as Nelson & Company. During the year 1857, Nelson and Ismay decided to create a shipbroking business together. This partnership became known as Nelson, Ismay & Company, but as Thomas was under 21 years of age, the articles of agreement could not be signed until January of the following year.

Together, they took offices in Drury Buildings, 21 Water Street, Liverpool. Nelson was extremely cautious in all he did, whereas Ismay was full of youthful enthusiasm for the very latest design in ships. Iron in shipbuilding was not yet popular, but the youthful Thomas was convinced that the day would come when practically all ships would be built of iron.

Two years into the partnership, they commissioned their first ship, *Angelita*. Registered in 1859, *Angelita* was built by Alexander Stephen & Sons, a Scottish company specialising in the development of steam power and the use of iron for ship-building. *Angelita* was a small brigantine of 134 tonnes, which proved profitable for the company, with orders being placed the following year for two larger vessels, *Mexico*, a 187-ton schooner, and *Ismay*, a 447-ton barque. It was Ismay's insistence that all three ships would be iron-built, and eventually – with some reluctance – Nelson agreed. The three new ships were built at Stephenson's Kelvinhaugh yard in Glasgow and given the yard numbers 21, 29 and 30.

However, at the beginning of 1862, following the loss of *Angelita*, Nelson and Ismay decided they could no longer work together, and the partnership was dissolved by mutual consent on the first day of April 1862. Thomas agreed to take responsibility for all debts due to and owed by the firm. When the partnership with Nelson ended, Thomas moved his business to 10 Water Street, Liverpool and became known as T.H. Ismay & Company.

Around the time that the order had been placed for *Angelita*, Thomas met Margaret, the eldest daughter of ship owners Luke and Mary Bruce. They fell in love almost immediately, and it was a love that was to last throughout their whole lives. They married on 7 April 1859 at St Bride's Church, Percy Street, Liverpool. It was by no coincidence that this was also the wedding anniversary of Thomas' father and mother.

Thomas and Margaret were blessed with five daughters and four sons, one of whom, Henry Sealby Ismay, died at only eighteen months. Their eldest son, Joseph Bruce Ismay, was destined to succeed his father as head of the White Star Line and to become infamous to many as the man who left

RMS *Titanic*, as the ship slipped beneath the icy waters of the North Atlantic.

Margaret, or Maggie, as Thomas called her, was a wonderful wife and mother. She supported her husband in all that he did, and the couple were perfectly devoted; each lived for the other and for their children.

3

PURCHASE OF THE WHITE STAR LINE

Thomas Henry Ismay, now a director of the National Line, purchased the name flag and the goodwill of the White Star Line in 1867 for £1,000. The line was originally owned by Henry Threllfall Wilson and John Pilkington, but in 1863 Pilkington left the company to be replaced by James Chambers, also from Cumbria, who had commissioned the company's first steamship, *Royal Standard*.

After two years' trading, mainly on the Australian route, Thomas was approached by Liverpool merchant Gustavus Schwabe, who explained that his nephew, Gustav Wilhelm Wolff had recently partnered with Mr Edward Harland for the purpose of shipbuilding in Belfast and had recently built some iron ships of a revolutionary design. Schwabe was already a large shareholder in this company but had been told that no more shares were available. Being anxious to invest more money into shipping, he suggested to Thomas Ismay that he was the ideal man to start a new company of steamships, mainly to work the North Atlantic trade.

Schwabe said that if Ismay would agree to have the steamships built by Harland & Wolff, he would back the scheme without exception, and persuade other Liverpool businessmen he knew to do the same. So, in 1869, the Oceanic Steam Navigation Company was formed, with a capital of £400,000, of which Thomas subscribed a large percentage. Other shareholders included Edward James Harland and Gustav Wilhelm Wolff.

Harland & Wolff were immediately commissioned to build four ships, the first of which was *Oceanic*, followed by *Atlantic*, *Baltic* and *Republic*. These original steamers were all of similar design, with such improvements as were found necessary through the experience gained by their use in service. The order was later increased to six ships, the additional two being *Adriatic* and *Celtic*, which were 17ft longer.

With the appearance of *Oceanic* in the Mersey, the old liners looked outdated, as the new ships were long and narrow, appearing more like a yacht than an Atlantic liner. The design was completely revolutionary. The old high bulwarks had completely disappeared and were replaced by iron railings so that the sea could flow freely from the deck. The deckhouses had gone, and the decks were built out to the full width of the ship for the first time.

These designs were Edward Harland's, but on seeing them, Thomas Ismay suggested several alterations which Harland & Wolff instantly incorporated. He suggested moving the main saloon and all First Class accommodation amidships, where the vibration from the engines would be least noticeable. He also suggested that cabins should be given a larger porthole, thereby making them bright and airy.

Oceanic and her sister ships made all other Atlantic steamships appear outdated almost overnight. Once again, Thomas had set new standards for ocean-going liners, and under his control, the company was set to become a world leader.

This was the beginning of the wonderful partnership that existed between White Star Line and Harland & Wolff. The heads of each of the firms became personal friends and a mutual trust and respect began to grow. With the exception of just one ship, *Laurentic* (II), the ships were all built on a cost-plus basis, with a percentage of the total build cost added, which was the builder's profit.

Harland & Wolff were given absolute freedom to design and construct the finest possible ships, which they did exceedingly well. No other shipbuilder would receive a White Star contract, while Harland & Wolff agreed not to build ships for any firm that was in direct competition with the White Star Line. It was an agreement that worked very well for both the White Star Line and Harland & Wolff.

Following the death of William Imrie in 1870, his son, also named William, a close friend of Thomas for over fifteen years, transferred the whole of Imrie Tomlinson to T.H. Ismay & Company. Instantly the firm became known as Ismay, Imrie & Company and became a subsidiary of the Oceanic Steam Navigation Company. The head office of Ismay, Imrie & Company remained at 10 Water Street until the new offices at 30 James Street were completed in 1898.

Thomas wished to ensure that his passengers would experience the best possible crossing while on board his vessels. In consequence, he prepared a letter which would, while Thomas was head of the line, be given to every captain upon accepting command of a White Star vessel. This example was sent to Captain Digby Murray on taking command of *Oceanic*, on her maiden voyage from Liverpool to New York, on 2 March 1871:

Captain Digby Murray
February 1871.

Dear Sir,

When placing the Steamer Oceanic under your charge, we endeavoured to impress upon you verbally, and in the most forcible manner we were capable of, the paramount and vital importance above all other things, of caution in the navigation of your vessel, and we now confirm this in writing, begging you to remember that the safety of your passengers and crew weigh with us, above and before all other considerations. We invite you also to bear in mind that while using due diligence in making a favourable passage to dismiss from your mind all idea of competitive passages with other vessels, concentrating your whole attention upon a cautious, prudent, and ever watchful system of navigation, which shall lose time, or suffer any other temporary inconvenience, rather than run the slightest risk which can be avoided. We are aware that, in the American Trade where quick passages are so much spoken of you will naturally feel a desire that your ship shall compare favourably with others in this respect, and this being so we deem it our duty to say to you most emphatically that, under no circumstances, can we sanction any system of navigation which involves the least risk or danger.

We request you to make an invariable practice of being yourself on deck when the weather is thick or obscure, in all narrow waters, and whenever the ship is within 60 miles of land; also to keep the lead going in either of the last mentioned cases, this being, in our opinion, a measure of the greatest importance, and of undoubted utility.

We attach much importance also to giving a wide berth to all headlands, shallow waters, and other positions involving possible peril, and we recommend you to take cross bearings where practicable when approaching the land, and where this is not feasible you will then do well to take casts of the deep sea lead, which will assist in determining your locality.

The most rigid discipline on the part of your officers should be observed, whom you will exhort to avoid at all times convivial intercourse with passengers, or with each other, and only such an amount of communication with the former as is demanded by a necessary and business-like courtesy. We must also remind you that it is essential to successful navigation that the crew be kept under judicious control; that the lookout be zealously watched, and required to report themselves in a loud and unmistakable voice after each bell sounds, as in this way you have a check upon their watchfulness.

We have full confidence in your sobriety of habit, but we may nevertheless exhort you to abstain from stimulants altogether, whilst on board ship (except in so far as the requirements of health may demand) endeavouring at the same time to imbue your officers, and all those about you, with a due sense of the advantage which will accrue not only to the Company, but to themselves, by being strictly temperate, as this quality will weigh with us in a special manner when giving promotion.

The consumption of coals, stores and provisions and indeed all articles constituting the equipment for the voyage should engage your daily attention, and so far as possible at a regular fixed hour, in order that you may be forewarned of any deficiency which may be impending, and that waste may be avoided, and a limitation in quantity determined on while it is yet time to avail of this expedient. The vessels of the Company have always been hitherto, and will be so long as the direction is in our hands provided with a full and complete outfit under these various heads, but where waste and thoughtless extravagance occur on the part of those in charge of any of the departments, it will be your duty to check such reckless and dangerous proceedings, and take measures to bring about an immediate change. We count upon your reporting to us without fear or favour all instances of incapacity or irregularity on the part of your officers or others under your control, as in this way only can we determine upon their respective merits, and hope to surround you with an efficient and reliable staff.

After having thus dwelt somewhat minutely upon matters of detail connected with your command, it may not be unprofitable to impress you with a deep sense of the injury which the interest of this Company would sustain in the event of any misfortune attending the navigation of your vessel:-

First. From the blow which such would give to the reputation of the line.

Second. From the pecuniary loss which would accrue the Company being their own insurers to a very large extent: and

Third. To the interruption of a regular service upon which much of the success of the present organisation must depend.

We may also state that, if at any time you have any suggestions to make, bearing upon the steamers; their outfit; or any matter connected with them and the trade, we shall at all times be glad to receive, and consider such.

We have alluded to such points as have occurred to us regarding this subject of safe and watchful navigation, and we need scarcely say to you, in conclusion, how deeply the question affects not only the well-being, but the very existence of the Company, and how earnestly we ask for your co-operation in achieving that success which can only be obtained by prudence and watchfulness at all times, whether in the presence of danger, or when by its absence you may be lured into a false sense of security.

It is the opinion of many that, where there is apparently least peril, there is most danger, and we incline to think that this remark is nearer the truth than is often thought to be the case.

Wishing you every success in your new command, we are,

Yours faithfully,

Ismay, Imrie & Company.

Almost one year later, Captain Digby Murray found himself in command of SS *Republic* during her maiden voyage from Liverpool to New York, sailing on 2 February 1872, with the ship experiencing extremely bad weather throughout most of the crossing. While being mindful of the letter he received from his employers one year earlier, he wrote a report of the voyage, expressing his thoughts on improvements that he, as captain, felt necessary. The report was sent to Ismay, Imrie & Company the moment they reached New York.

Throughout most of *Republic*'s maiden voyage, the ship encountered particularly poor weather conditions with exceptionally high winds. Captain Murray was deeply concerned about water leaking into the upper decks, which continued for several days, causing flooding in the saloon and staterooms. He was also deeply concerned that the wheelhouse windows had been broken by the waves and the ship's compass became detached from its mounting and smashed, along with other equipment within the wheelhouse. Three lifeboats had also been damaged by waves breaking over the deck, while the cover of a forward ventilator had been washed away, causing a great deal of water to wash down the companionway, flooding the women's quarters aft.

Captain Murray also described the additional work undertaken by the ship's crew in order to minimise damage. This left no time for crew members to attend many of their regular duties, with the ship's officers and remaining crew becoming worn out. It was Murray's opinion that the new ship was too deep in the water for that time of the year, suggesting that there should be guidance regarding loading of ships on the North Atlantic service between the months of November through to April. The ability to handle *Republic* in such bad weather also left the crew unable to secure the quarterdeck lifeboats, despite having all hands on deck since Queenstown.

Murray further wrote about the handling of the ship in poor sea conditions, describing the ship as dipping her stern into the sea frequently and very heavily, and further explaining that there was so much weight in her fore end that it gave her no chance to rise and, though he had the will, he was quite unable to drive her.

Seven days into the voyage they were fortunate to see a brief respite in the weather, but the following day a terrific gale blew up again, this time destroying all but two lifeboats. At the same time, the engine-room skylight was smashed, falling on top of the steam-driven cylinders below, followed by large amounts of water which almost extinguished the boiler fires. Captain Murray felt that the skylight had never been properly secured.

Second Officer Williams was busy attempting to cover the opening using a sail when he was struck by No. 4 lifeboat, which had been swinging on the davits when it was hit by a huge wave, destroying the boat and thrusting debris toward Officer Williams. As a result, Williams suffered broken ribs, broken upper left leg and a dislocated ankle.

Fearing that the ship would lose steam, Murray ordered a sail to be set but this was never deployed. Soon afterwards, a large sea wash struck the mizzen boom, which would have been disastrous had the sail been set. Thanks to the quick thinking of the engine-room crew, *Republic* was able to generate a small amount of steam, enough to move forward at a speed of between 1 and 2 knots.

Murray was hugely critical of the external doorways, going so far as to suggest that if improvements were not made, then it would be inevitable that a ship would be lost. Water had found its way into other parts of the ship, including the icehouse and the galley, preventing any food being cooked for almost three days. In other parts of the ship, carpets and paintwork had been ruined. The majority of rails on the promenade deck had been swept away, telegraphs were broken, and the top of the standard binnacle along with the forward gangway were washed overboard. The large ventilator and three davits were also gone, with many doors, windows and shutters being destroyed.

However, despite all these setbacks, Captain Murray was full of praise for the ship's power plant, steering mechanisms and strength of the hull. He also made reference to the bravery, strength and resilience of the majority of the ship's crew.

Later the same year, Thomas Henry Ismay was becoming anxious about several reports he had received from Mr Joseph Hyde Sparks, White Star's agent in New York. Mr Sparks had received complaints from steerage passengers, referring to the conditions aboard their vessels. This concerned Thomas greatly. He wished to have a first-hand account of steerage conditions on his ships, so after careful consideration, he conceived the idea of sending out a trustworthy member of his staff to travel to New York as a steerage passenger aboard SS *Oceanic*. This would need to be someone with whom the officers and crew members were unacquainted. Consequently, the following letter was sent to Mr Sparks:

September 25th, 1872.
J. Hyde Sparks, Esq.,
New York.

Dear Sir,

Referring to your remarks regarding the complaint from Steerage Passengers, we are of the opinion that much as we have already done for their comfort, there is still room for further improvement without incurring additional expense, and being anxious to have some report upon which we can depend and act, we have decided to send Captain Hinds out in the present steamer as a Steerage Passenger, so that on his return he may be able to report to us from actual experience, and from his report we may be able to judge what are the best means to adopt in the future.

His trip is unknown to anyone in the office here, you will, therefore, please keep the knowledge of his visit from any of your staff. Captain Hinds is a stranger in New York. You will therefore please advise him as to where he should stay, and advance him what money he may require up to £20 debiting the same to us.

As to his return, we leave it with you to send him back either by one of our own boats, or in such manner as you think best.

We are, dear Sir,

Yours truly, Ismay, Imrie & Co.[1]

After receiving Captain Hinds' report, Ismay, Imrie & Co. took drastic measures and conditions, especially in steerage, were greatly improved.

By 1881 the White Star Line was proving very profitable – so profitable that the shareholders wished to show their appreciation to Thomas Ismay and William Imrie by seeking to have the articles of agreement altered, in order that Ismay and Imrie could take a larger commission, but neither of them would agree to it. The shareholders desperately wanted to show their appreciation and suggested that Thomas Ismay should sit for a portrait at the studio of Mr John Millais, later known as Sir John Millais. They also commissioned Hunt and Roskell to make a silver-gilt dinner service that, upon completion, was valued at 3,000 guineas. Two years later, and after several sittings, the portrait was complete. Thomas was invited to a private viewing at the Royal Academy. His wife Margaret made the following entry in her diary:

> May 4th, Friday, 1883. At the Private View at the Academy. Sarah went with us. Quite a number of friends, Thomas' picture by Millais hung on the line. Many opinions respecting it, principally that it does not do him justice. I don't like the expression.

In September 1885, a dinner was held aboard *Adriatic* while she was moored in Liverpool. During dinner, the shareholders presented Mr Ismay with the portrait by Millais and also the silver dinner service. Mr Imrie was presented with some pictures that he had chosen previously. The presentations were made in recognition of the work the two partners had done over the years.

In addition to all this, there was a leatherbound book that had been printed especially for the occasion. The following description appeared in the book:

> An interesting and pleasant gathering took place on Wednesday evening September 16th, onboard the R.M.S. Adriatic when about 70 shareholders in the Oceanic Steam Navigation Company, better known as the White Star Line, (of which Messrs. Ismay, Imrie Company are the Managing Owners) together with various heads of departments of the firm, making in all about 100 guests, partook of dinner. Previous to the presentation to Mr. Ismay of a valuable

service of plate designed and manufactured by Messrs. Hunt & Roskell of London, and his portrait, by Sir J. Millais R.A. and to Mr. Imrie of two pictures selected by himself, one entitled, Melittion by Sir Frederick Leighton, P.R.A. and the other The Feast of Pomona by Lawrence Alma-Tadema, R.A. The service of plate presented to Mr. Ismay is in silver gilt, and consists of a centre piece, four candelabra, two oval flower stands, four round and two oval fruit stands, two sugar vases and ladles, two claret or water jugs, four goblets, and twelve salt cellars, and spoons. The various pieces have been designed to illustrate the progress of the art of navigation from the earliest times to the present day, its means and objects. The centre piece is a magnificent illustration of the art of modelling in silver and the designer and modeller being Mr. G. A. Carter.

On this piece, and occupying the central position of the whole service, is a globe with tin-seas and continents marked upon it. Round it are seated figures of four of the chief navigators associated with Discovery; Jason, as leader of the earliest recorded expedition across the seas; Vasco da Gama, the discoverer of the route to India by doubling the Cape; Columbus; and Captain Cook. The base is ornamented with four small groups symbolical of the wind and of the sea and its attributes. At the angles of the plinth supporting the globe are four small groups typical of the four continents.

The lower moulding of this and of all the other pieces in tin-Service is enriched with the Greek Wave, a symbol of the sea, the base from which the subject – Navigation – springs. Other mouldings are formed of shells, cables, etc. Upon two of the four panels behind the figures of the great navigators are engraved the official seal of the Oceanic Steam Navigation Co. and Mr. Ismay's crest, and upon the other two appears the following inscription:

The Service of Plate, of which this is the centre, is presented to Thomas Henry Ismay, Esquire by the Shareholders of the White Star Line, in token of the esteem in which he is held by them, and in recognition of the fact that to the sound judgment, untiring energy, and singleness of purpose he has displayed in the management of their affairs for the past fifteen years, the prosperity of the Company is mainly due.

Dinner was served at five, and the guests included family, friends and shareholders. After dinner was over, several speeches followed, the first of which was made by Mr Thomas Jackson.

Some of our friends who have not had the opportunity of attending the Annual Meetings of the Company may desire to know what has led to our assembling today in special honour to our Managers. It may, therefore, be well if I refer to the Annual Meeting held on the 23rd February, 1881. The suggestion which has brought us together arose from the fact that circumstances had considerably changed from the time when the Company was formed and the original Articles of Association were framed. It was suggested and resolved unanimously that the Articles should be so altered as to give the Managers a larger commission than they were then receiving; but when the proposal was made, Mr. Ismay, on behalf of his firm, at once refused to accept any further remuneration and added, that for better or worse, he was content with the existing arrangements. It was then proposed and adopted with the utmost cordiality, that some special acknowledgment, not only of the Manager's self-denial in refusing that offer, but of the excellent way in which they had managed the Company's property, should be made. A Committee was accordingly formed to ask Mr. Ismay to sit for a portrait of himself by Sir J. E. Millais, which portrait I have no doubt a good many of you have seen at the Royal Academy in London and to accept a Service of Plate, by Hunt & Roskell; and to present Mr. Imrie with two oil paintings to be selected by himself. Now, ladies and gentlemen, naturally some of you will ask how does it come about that so long a time as four years has elapsed between the appointment of the Committee and the completion of their duty? There are many reasons. Mr. Ismay has had to sit for his portrait, which took some time; and I think you will see that such a design as that before you in the Service of Plate could not be obtained in a day, and after it was obtained to have it carefully executed required a much longer time than some of us calculated on. Further, I think that Mr. Ismay himself has wished to delay this presentation, in the hope that the general shipping trade might improve, and we should then meet together under still more favourable auspices.

The Company has had to fight its way from the beginning against the keenest competition, and we have attained a position which I feel we may be all very justly proud of today. We have, out of our original capital built 64,000 tons of shipping, which have cost over two million sterling; and we have now, in addition to our Atlantic Fleet, of which this noble ship we are in is a specimen, the Coptic, Ionic, Doric, Belgic, Gaelic, Oceanic and Arabic, in all 55,033 tons of shipping such as there is not to be found in any part of the world.

Now, I am sure it would not be Mr. Ismay's wish that I should enter upon any fulsome eulogy of his services, but I must take it upon myself to say, not only from my intimate knowledge of Mr. Ismay, but of business in Liverpool generally, that we owe the largest share of our prosperity to him. He has gone into every detail of our work. He has been approachable by everybody great and small, and he has shown a wonderful power of discrimination in finding out the right man for the right place. I may remark also, that we owe not a little to Mr. Ismay's coolness and good judgment into not being led into following in the wake of those who have rushed into large and costly steamers. I do not know what his views as to the future may be, for he has a knack of keeping them to himself, but this I may safely predict, that when he thinks the time has come to build larger and faster boats we as Shareholders, shall be safe in his hands, for he will consider our interests before either the profit or the fame of the managers. I would also mention this in regard to Mr. Ismay that he has travelled far and wide in the interest of the Company. He has not been satisfied to let ships go abroad without knowing where and to whom they were going and the character of the trade in which they were employed. I now simply ask Mr. Ismay and Mr. Imrie to receive from the Shareholders these tokens of their affection and esteem and with best wishes from us all.

Two years later, at the age of 50, which was also the year of Queen Victoria's Golden Jubilee, Thomas decided to mark the jubilee year by setting up a pension fund for Liverpool seamen, whether retired through age or ill health. He sent the following letter to Thomas William Oakshott, Mayor of Liverpool:

Dawpool
Thurstaston
Birkenhead
June 4th 1887

Dear Mr. Mayor,
    The forthcoming celebration of the 50th Anniversary of Her Majesty Queen Victoria's accession to the throne of England is an event of the widest significance, in-as-much

as it not only serves to remind us of the many blessings which have been bestowed upon the nation during her long and prosperous reign, but it also affords exceptional opportunity to those who may have been favoured to testify their thankfulness, by giving help to projects for the promotion of the welfare and happiness of their less favoured fellow countrymen.

Liverpool, as the greatest seaport in the world, has a numerous sea-faring population, amongst whom, much distress exists, frequently from circumstances beyond their control, and whilst considerable assistance has been rendered to the sailor's widows and orphans, beyond the building and partial endowment of the excellent home at Egremont, comparatively little has been done for the sailor himself. Provident Societies are not available for him, as in the case of other labouring classes employed in less hazardous trades and occupations ashore, and the old or distressed sailor who has failed to make provision for his declining years, has too often to rely upon the uncertain assistance of his relatives and friends, or – dread necessity – seek admission to the Work House.

With the object of relieving such cases I would suggest the establishment of a fund on the outlines of the enclosed memorandum, to be called The Liverpool Seamen's Pension Fund, towards which I should be pleased in acknowledgment of the completion of my fiftieth year to contribute £20,000, and from the interest of which pensions of £20 per annum may be granted to old and worn out Liverpool sailors. I do not propose that this fund shall be numbered amongst the already long list of charities seeking subscriptions as their principle means of support, but donations or bequests would naturally extend its sphere of usefulness, and it will be managed without expense of any kind, and the whole of the income derived from it will be applied to the object which I have in view.

> Believe me, dear Mr. Mayor,
> Yours very truly,
> Thomas H. Ismay[2]

Soon after Thomas' letter to the mayor was sent, he had the following memorandum drawn up:

MEMORANDUM OF ENTITLEMENT
The object of the fund is to provide pensions for British sailors who have sailed out of Liverpool, or in Liverpool owned ships, and who have been unable to make adequate provision for their declining years.

The pension, which it is proposed shall be fixed at £20 per year will not be granted to any person other than a British sailor and will be continued at the absolute discretion of the Committee.

No person should be eligible for the pension who is able to serve at sea, or who has not attained the age of 50 years.

Those persons only will be admitted as candidates who can prove 25 years of service at sea in the Mercantile Marine as Captain, Deck Officer or Seaman.

The fund may be vested in the name of the Mercantile Marine Service Association, who will have the power of selecting suitable candidates for the pension.'

Two years later, Thomas and Margaret decided to visit his hometown of Maryport. Thomas' mother, Mary, had died in 1869 at just 63 years of age. She had died intestate; therefore, all her property was passed to her eldest son Thomas, including the house in Whillans Yard in which he was born and Ropery House, to which the family had moved when Thomas was 6 years of age.

He sold the house at Whillans Yard to his younger brother, John Sealby Ismay, selling Ropery House a short time later.

While visiting Maryport, Mr and Mrs Ismay stayed with the Senhouse family at Netherhall Mansion. It may be assumed that they visited the two properties in which Thomas spent his childhood. However, their time in Maryport was short, and Margaret made no mention of the properties in her diary. They were able to visit Mr John Cockton, a close friend of Thomas since their childhood days in Maryport. Later in life, Mr Cockton became a chemist in the town and supplied much of the pharmaceutical equipment for Ismay, Imrie & Co. He also held a small number of shares in the White Star Line.

Thomas never forgot the town in which he was born. He also loved the townsfolk, many of whom he remembered from his childhood there. It had been said that if a Maryport man turned up at the White Star Line offices, he would be guaranteed a job. In December 1876, Thomas set up a fund for the old people of the town. This took the form of £5 for coal and £20 for blankets, to be distributed every Christmas. In the following year, a further £25 was added to the fund; this was to include a shilling's worth of groceries for every person every week. Thomas made provision for this fund to continue until long after his death.

Some ten years previous to this visit, T.H. Ismay had heard that Christ Church, next to the harbour, needed a new clock for the spire. Understanding the importance of a clock facing all four points of the compass, especially facing west and therefore being visible from the sea and the port, he immediately had one installed, the work being completed in 1878. This clock can still be seen there today, although the church is in a poor state of repair. He also provided assistance for other local churches, one such example being St Mary's, Maryport. In this church, Thomas paid for new stained-glass windows as the original ones were damaged by a storm. Again, these windows can be seen today; they bear the inscription:

> This window is dedicated to the glory of God, and the grateful memory of Joseph Ismay and Mary his wife, by their son Thomas Henry Ismay.

Margaret Ismay recorded their visit to Maryport:

> September 24th, Tuesday, 1889. Left Liverpool with Thomas by 11:35 a.m. train for Maryport to open a bazaar there tomorrow. We are staying with Mr Senhouse at Netherhall.

> September 25th, Wednesday. Thomas and I walked up some of the old streets, and then called at Mr. Cockton's and went to see the lifeboat launched, then walked back to Netherhall. Lunched at 1 p.m. and started for the Bazaar at 2 p.m. Large number at the opening. Thomas delivered his remarks nicely, bought a few things, had tea at Netherhall and left for Liverpool by 6 p.m. train.

At this time, unemployment was high, so T.H. Ismay had some unemployed men from Liverpool transported to Dawpool, where he employed them to weed the heather. He took the view that it was much better for their self-respect to be given a job to do, rather than to live on charity.

In 1890 he was made High Sheriff of Cheshire, a position he enjoyed for two consecutive years, and one of his duties was to attend the County Assizes. The whole family went to see T.H. Ismay in his sheriff's robes with his sheriff's carriage; Mrs Ismay was very sorry when his term of office came to an end.

At the end of his second year in the sheriff's office, T.H. Ismay's son James married Lady Margaret Seymour, the eldest daughter of the Marquis of Hertford. It was a marriage of which Thomas did not fully approve as he felt that he and his family were business-people, and therefore should not be marrying into the aristocracy. Despite his original misgivings, Thomas quickly became very fond of his new daughter-in-law and accepted the marriage. The newlyweds took residence at Caldy Manor, some 2 miles to the north-west of Dawpool.

During the summer, James arranged a cricket match on the playing field near Dawpool. In addition to cricket matches with local teams, the Dawpool cricket club played matches against the young men of the training ship, HMS *Conway*. Thomas had always taken a keen interest in *Conway*, and he, along with members of his family, attended the prizegiving ceremonies on board. Despite this, Thomas never held the same enthusiasm as he did with TS *Indefatigable*, a training ship that he had helped to found for poor boys, to assist them in obtaining a good start in life.

In April the following year, Mr and Mrs Ismay took their two daughters, Ethel and Ada, to America aboard *Majestic*, as they had been invited to attend the opening of the prestigious Chicago World Fair. This was the first time the two sisters, now aged 13 and 11, had journeyed to the USA. The girls had heard so much about America and on arrival found it to exceed all their expectations, thoroughly enjoying every moment there. Mr William Seaward Webb arranged for a private railway coach to be attached to the train which took them from New York to Chicago.

The family returned to New York two weeks later, calling at Washington to meet President Cleveland at the White House. On their return to New York, the family spent several days with their daughter-in-law's parents, George and Julia Schieffelin, before returning to Liverpool aboard *Teutonic*.

By 1892, Thomas had officially retired from the firm of Ismay, Imrie & Co. but remained as chairman, keeping a great interest in the company and its affairs, and his decision on most things was final. This gave him more time to pursue his interests with several boards on which he served and many charities in which he took a special interest. He became president of the Royal Infirmary and donated £1,000, the purpose being to start an endowment fund. At about the same time, he took 200 children from a school for deaf children to Liverpool dock for a one-day cruise aboard the White Star liner *Teutonic*.

Meanwhile, the White Star liner *Germanic* had been returned to the shipbuilders in Belfast for refurbishment, returning to service in May 1895. She now returned to Liverpool after having been re-engineered with a triple-expansion steam engine. Thomas and his eldest son Bruce were on board *Germanic* when the ship returned to Liverpool so that they could witness at first hand the improvements that had been made, and they were delighted. Mrs Ismay recorded the event in her diary:

> May 13th, Monday, 1895. Ethel and I went in by the 10 a.m. train to see the Germanic. She has been beautifully done up. New engines, boilers, etc., and looks well. She sails for New York Wednesday next. Then onboard Oceanic to lunch. It is 15 years since we went out to Japan in her, and she has not been in England since. I looked upon her as my favourite ship but she disappointed me.

One of the great drawbacks to the Liverpool–New York crossing was the absence of a convenient connecting railway on the Liverpool side, but in July of the same year, a new station was opened. Mrs Ismay was present for the occasion and wrote in her diary:

> July 10th, Wednesday, 1895. The Riverside Station for Atlantic passengers formally opened, Thomas responded to the toast,

'Success to the Atlantic trade' and made to my thinking a most excellent speech. The Mersey Docks and Harbour Board gave a large luncheon, Lord Stalbridge and several of the LNWR [London and North Western Railway] Directors came down by special train. The Majestic came alongside the stage. Captain Smith in charge for the first time. [This was the same Smith who would later be captain of *Titanic*].

Later the same year, the family gathered at Dawpool for Christmas, but this year was not a joyful one. It was Christmas Eve when they heard of the sudden death of Sir Edward Harland at his Irish home, Glenfarne Hall, Leitrim, his cause of death being determined as heart disease. Thomas Ismay travelled to Glenfarne for his funeral, which took place on 28 December.

Thomas was very upset at the death of his close friend. For the past twenty-five years, they had worked together to build up a great enterprise, and the White Star Line owed its success, at least in part, to Sir Edward Harland for the magnificent ships his company had built for them. Thomas wished to make a permanent memorial for Sir Harland, so the following month, at the Engineer's Dinner, he asked the Lord Mayor to announce that it was the intention of the White Star Line to give £2,000 to the trustees of Liverpool University for a scholarship which would be called the Edward Harland Memorial Scholarship.

★★★

In 1897, Mr and Mrs Ismay had been visiting the London home of their daughter, Ethel, when Thomas received a letter from Mr Schomberg Kerr McDonnell, Principal Private Secretary to the Prime Minister. The letter was marked 'With reference to an important matter'. Mrs Ismay writes about this in her diary:

June 16th, Wednesday, 1897. Thomas went to the Foreign Office, and found that the Queen wishes to confer a Baronetcy on him, which is a great honour particularly as it comes from no political reason, but as recognition of good work done, and this being the 60th year of Her Majesty's reign. Causes him to waver as to whether he ought to accept. Mrs. Wilberforce lunched here and strongly urged him to accept.

June 17, Thursday, 1897. Thomas wired for Bruce to come up. He got here at 9 a.m. and we discussed this proposed honour. He was quite agreeable for Thomas to do what he thought best, but from the first Thomas felt that he would rather decline. I am proud he has been offered a Baronetcy, but think he will be happier to remain as he began.

Despite positive advice from his friends and colleagues, and after much deliberation with his family, Thomas decided to decline this gracious offer. Again, Mrs Ismay records the following:

June 18th, Friday, 1897. Thomas went to Euston and sent his letter to Mr. Schomberg McDonnell declining the honour the Queen wished to confer on him. I think he will feel the happier for it and be better satisfied at remaining Mr. Ismay than if he had been Sir Thomas.

The following is the letter mentioned:

The Board Room,
Euston Station.
June 18th, 1897.

Dear Mr. MacDonnell,

With regard to our conversation of yesterday, after giving the matter referred to my most careful and anxious consideration, I have come to the conclusion, that while deeply grateful to Her Majesty for thinking of conferring such an honour upon me, I feel it will be better most respectfully to decline the very flattering proposal. Will you please convey to the Prime Minister my appreciation of the terms on which he conveyed to you the Queen's gracious message, and my regret that I am unable to fall in with his wishes. May I add that I hope Lord Salisbury will understand the spirit in which this letter is written, and thank you personally for your kind expressions.

Believe me,

Yours sincerely,

Thomas H. Ismay

Meanwhile, Harland & Wolff had been drawing up plans for two new ships to sail the Liverpool–New York service. They were to be called *Oceanic*, named after the pioneer vessel of the line, and *Olympic*. They were to be the largest and most luxurious vessels in the world.

In July of 1898, Thomas and Margaret visited Belfast to see the interior of the first of the new ships. They were impressed with some of the interior decorations, particularly the library, but overall, they were not entirely satisfied, so Thomas made the decision to call in George Trollope & Company, and also to call on the advice of Mr Norman Shaw. Throughout the year, several consultations took place between George Trollope & Company, Mr Shaw and Mr and Mrs Ismay in order to decide on the interior decorations for *Oceanic*.

However, while work on *Oceanic* continued, plans for the sister ship *Olympic* were shelved due to Thomas' declining health. It would be more than a decade before a ship would be given that name.

The White Star Line moved into new offices on the last day of 1897. Mr Shaw had designed the offices at 30 James Street, Liverpool. The exterior of the building closely resembled New Scotland Yard, which he had also designed.

In January of the New Year, Mrs Ismay went to inspect the new offices, and she recorded her thoughts:

> January 29th, Saturday, 1898. The carriage came for me at 10.30, I called at the Office and went all over them with Jimmy. They look very businesslike, but I miss the cosiness of the old ones, and don't quite like where Mr. Imrie is.

Mr Imrie did not have an office to himself, but instead was given an alcove in the corner of one of the main offices, which was curtained off.

★★★

In January 1899, Thomas and Margaret Ismay crossed to Queenstown on *Teutonic*, and from there travelled to Belfast to witness the launching of *Oceanic*, which Mrs Ismay describes:

> January 14th, Saturday, 1899. Mr. Pirrie left for the yard at 6 o'clock, Thomas at 9 and Mrs. Pirrie and I at 10. The Oceanic was safely launched at about 11.20 a.m. A most beautiful sight it was to see the noble ship, glide so gracefully into the water. May she be all that we could wish.

This was the last launch that Thomas would attend. He had planned to be aboard *Oceanic* on her maiden voyage to New York, but this was to be a crossing he would never make.

4

Declining Health

Thomas had been in good health for almost all his life, but his last months were far from healthy. By the beginning of 1899, shortly after *Oceanic* was launched, he began to suffer from pains in his chest. He quickly became so ill that his family and friends began to worry over his long-term health.

By the end of March, Thomas felt well enough to take a short break. He and Margaret travelled to Windermere, which is located on the southern edge of the English Lake District. They had stayed there soon after they were married and had vowed that they would return. While in Windermere, Thomas began to suffer from severe pains. Mrs Ismay made the following entry in her diary:

April 3rd, Monday, 1899. Thomas was seized with a violent pain at the bottom of the bowel; I got him to bed, applied a hot fomentation, and sent for the doctor, who gave him a dose of morphia.

The pain was diagnosed as appendicitis, and the doctor advised Mr Ismay that it would be wise not to travel for several days.

They returned home to Dawpool three days later, by which time Thomas was feeling much better, but by the time they reached Dawpool, Thomas was beginning to feel unwell again. They had planned a dinner at the Royal Academy on 26 April, and Thomas was determined to attend, although this would necessitate a stay overnight in London.

Once they returned to Liverpool, Margaret summoned the doctor again. Upon examination, he found the gall duct to be considerably enlarged and diagnosed the problem as gall stones. Thomas was determined to keep his prior engagements, including attending a meeting with the Oceanic Steam Navigation Company the following month and a meeting in London with the London and North Western Railway.

In July of the same year, Thomas and his family travelled to Belfast to witness *Oceanic* nearing completion, and also for Thomas to receive the Freedom of the City of Belfast.

The following month Thomas collapsed again, just as the now completed *Oceanic* was due to be seen in the Mersey. It was a distressing time for all his family. Thomas had wished to travel to America aboard his newest ship, but it was now becoming apparent that his illness was far more serious than anyone had initially thought.

It became obvious that Thomas was not well enough to make the journey he had longed for. Nevertheless, he insisted on visiting *Oceanic* while he was able to do so. He stayed aboard for only forty-five minutes and was delighted with the new ship, but the effort proved too much. Margaret was becoming increasingly worried and sought the advice of a liver specialist. Consequently, Mr Mayo Robson of Leeds arrived at midnight, and after an examination, he advised that an operation would be necessary and that it could only be undertaken with the use of cocaine.

The operation was carried out at the family home on 31 August. The surgeon found a large abscess in the gall duct, this was removed, and the operation was considered successful. His two eldest sons, Joseph Bruce and James Hainsworth, remained at Dawpool until the operation was over.

Thomas' recovery was poor. Four days later, Mr Robson decided that another operation was necessary, but this time it would need to be performed under general anaesthetic and was carried out the same evening. The following morning, Thomas became very weak and seemed to realise that his time was short. He asked Margaret to arrange for prayers to be offered for him in St Bartholomew's Church.

The Emperor of Germany Wilhelm II was staying at Windsor Castle when he heard of Thomas' failing health, sending the following telegram to Mrs Ismay:

> Am most distressed at the news of the illness of your husband. I hope and trust that he may be spared to you, for he is one of the most prominent figures in the shipping world, and well known to me from the visit I once paid the Teutonic some years ago. Have just heard from a German gentleman who was a passenger on board the Oceanic that she is a marvel of perfection in building and fittings, and well worthy of the celebrated line and the illustrious owner she belongs to.

On 13 September, Thomas suffered the first of many heart attacks, which plagued him for over a month, and which finally took his life at 6.05 p.m. on 24 November 1899, in the fortieth year of their marriage, at only 62 years of age.

His dear wife was meticulous when keeping her diary and made the following entries during the time of Thomas' declining health:

> August 3rd, Thursday, 1899. Ada, Lottie, and I went to Liverpool to see the Medic which sails today for Australia.

Tim Fletcher is going out in her to the Cape. Thomas met us on board, he looks a shocking colour and I am sure another attack is coming.

August 4th, Friday, 1899. I sent for Dr. King and he finds his liver very much enlarged and heart weak.

August 5th, Saturday, 1899. Thomas had a very bad night indeed and is very poorly this morning. Bruce came to play in the cricket match and stay at Caldy until Monday.

August 23rd, Wednesday, 1899. Dr. King finds a distinct improvement in Thomas today, he got up at 11.30 and the Dr. says he thinks he will be well enough to go to Belfast on Friday, I sincerely hope he will. Bruce and Mr. Graves are leaving for Belfast today to join the Oceanic in the morning for her trials.

August 24th, Thursday, 1899. As Dr. King is afraid it is not prudent for Thomas to go to America in Oceanic, we decided to have another opinion – Dr. King suggested Dr. Barr, and after making a thorough examination, he also said it would not be desirable, as the liver is very much enlarged, and the movement would be bad for it. I am dreadfully sorry he should have this disappointment.

August 25th, Friday, 1899. The Oceanic sea trials were most satisfactory in every respect, yesterday Bruce sent frequent wires. Thomas has given up going to Belfast in the Magnetic.

August 26th, Saturday, 1899. Thomas drove to Birkenhead, went on board Magnetic and sailed out to meet Oceanic, he is very pleased with her, stayed on board for forty five minutes – Bruce drove back with him, I am thankful to say he feels no worse for his exertion.

August 28th, Monday, 1899. Thomas was so poorly this morning that I said he must have a specialist for the liver, after making enquiries in London and Liverpool we decided to send for Mr. Mayo Robson of Leeds. He got there at midnight and after examining Thomas he said that an operation would be necessary, but it only could be done with cocaine. Thomas consented and it was arranged for it to be done on Thursday morning.

August 31st, Thursday, 1899. Mr. Mayo Robson performed the operation this morning at 9 a.m. and found a large abscess had formed on the gall-duct, which he said was quite sufficient to account for all the pain Thomas suffered. He bore it bravely, but suffered very much. Mr Robson considers it a successful operation, God grant it may prove so. Bruce and Jimmy stayed until it was all over.

September 4th, Monday, 1899. Thomas so ill that Mr. Mayo Robson remained and saw him constantly during the day; I fear we are going from bad to worse. At 4.00 p.m. he said he feared another operation was necessary to relieve him, but it must be done under anaesthetics. Dr. Briggs administered it. Dr. Macrae got here at 8.30 and the operation was done at nine.

September 6th, Wednesday, 1899. Thomas not so well today, he had great pain all day and they were unable to give anything to relieve it. The Oceanic sailed from the river at 7 p.m. a very different sailing from what we expected. Mr. & Mrs. Pirrie went out in her – it is a great disappointment to

Thomas, but if he is only spared to recover, the other is of no importance; he also regrets that Bruce is not going.

Throughout the following weeks, Margaret continued to write her diary every day, where she recorded that her beloved husband's health was slowly becoming worse and began to suspect that he was unlikely to recover. Their children, including Bruce and his wife Florence, began spending more time with Thomas and Margaret, with the family continuing to attend church every Sunday, just as they always had. Near the end of November, Margaret made the following chilling entry in her diary, then continues to describe the following days:

November 23rd, Thursday, 1899. A very quiet night, having had a draught, from which he is very drowsy. Moved into my bed, but was only awake at intervals and took little nourishment. At 5.45 he had a severe tightness on his chest and my beloved one passed peacefully away at 3 minutes past six. I had his hand until they removed me.

November 24th, Friday, 1899. A terrible awakening. My loved one has gone. Mr. Imrie and Mr. Graves came round, also Mary, Captain Leslie and Mrs. Haddock.

November 26th, Sunday, 1899. The girls except Lottie went to church. Bruce, Florence and myself at home, the last Sunday I shall see him on earth, the day we loved so well.

November 27th, Monday, 1899. My beloved one laid to rest in Thurstaston Churchyard. The Bishop of Chichester assisted and I was given strength to attend. I wanted to follow them to the end. All seems gone now for me. A very large and representative gathering present and boys from the Indefatigable [training ship], Seamen's Orphanage, and Conway [training ship] – a sad day for me.

November 28th, Tuesday, 1899. There is a terrible, terrible blank in the house, shall we ever be able to live without him. All my life was centred in him, and as the time goes on it can only get worse for me.

Shortly before his death, Thomas received a letter from the New York office of Bradstreet, a respected American financial institution. This is possibly the last letter that he would read:

Mr Thomas H Ismay
Liverpool, England

My dear sir,

    I hand you under separate cover, a copy of the Proceedings and Resolutions of a meeting held September 12th, 1899, by the passengers who were fortunate as to sail on the maiden voyage of the 'Oceanic'. If such meetings of your patrons – embracing the most prominent and influential members of society and the business world – are of interest to you, it may be gratifying to know that in this particular instance the sentiments of the resolutions adopted reflect a personality so earnest and responsive on the part of those present as to assure you of the genuineness of their regard for your individual welfare and – in a broad sense – for all that concerns your great undertakings.

    I much regret that Mr. Jesup's absence from the city prevented the obtaining of his official signature to the proceedings.

    With assurances of the highest respect, I remain, dear Sir,

    Your obedient servant

    [Signed] Charles F. Clark

On the day of his death, the following detailed summary of Thomas' life appeared in *The Times* newspaper:

We regret to announce that Mr. Ismay died at his residence, Dawpool, near Birkenhead about 6 o'clock last night, after a long illness. The immediate cause of death was collapse of the heart, following on operations performed for an internal trouble. Doctor King, of West Kirby, the family physician, was present with several specialists.

Born on January 7, 1837, at Maryport, Cumberland, where his Father Joseph Ismay was a shipbuilder and ship-owner, Thomas Henry Ismay was educated at the Croft-house School, Carlisle. When Thomas reached 16 years of age he was apprenticed to Messers Imrie and Tomlinson, ship-owners and shipbrokers, Liverpool. After completing his indentures he widened his experience by travel, sailing around Cape Horn and visiting Chile, Peru, Bolivia. Returning to Liverpool, he started business on his own account; and in 1867, when but 30 years of age, he acquired the important of enterprise of the White Star Line of Australian clippers, which included White Star, Blue Jacket, Champion of the Seas and other sailing vessels famous in their day. In the following year Mr. Ismay, with former fellow-apprentice, Mr. William Imrie, formed the Oceanic Steam Navigation Company, Mr. Ismay, then devoting himself to the development of steam navigation. It was in 1870 that the firm decided upon entering into the competition for the Atlantic trade while still continuing the Australian, into which latter they had introduced steamers. Speaking on the occasion of the launch of the 'Oceanic' on January 14, 1899 Mr. Ismay said that he could not recall an unfriendly word in the course of a unique business relationship which began with the small sailing ship 'Broughton', of 600 tonnes in

1867, and has continued from that historic masterpiece of Sir Edward Harland's genius, the first 'Oceanic' – the pioneer steamship of the White Star line – without interruption to the present time, when the twin-screw steamer 'Oceanic' (2), of 17,000 tons, largest vessel afloat, represent, as we believe, the highest point of excellence ever attained in ship construction'. When the American service was commenced in 1870, the designation White Star Line was associated with it. Mr. Ismay's idea was that people considered safety and comfort as well as speed and he would not sacrifice these for the sake of making the first of passage. When the first 'Oceanic' was launched in 1871 she was the object of diverse criticism, but experience indicated her suitability for the trade for which she was built. The White Star Company rapidly developed in popularity, and their vessels have held high favour and among passengers, though they may not have been 'record breakers'. In the period covered by the remarks of Mr. Ismay above quoted no less than £7,000,000 was paid by the company for vessels built by Mesers Harland and Wolff. One of the earlier vessels to excite notice in this regard to speed (15 knots) was the 'Britannic', which made her first trip from New York in June 1874. The 'Majestic' and 'Teutonic' marked a great advance, and the 'Oceanic' illustrates still greater progress. While the passenger steamers have developed with requirements, cargo boats have also been provided for the future of the trade, including the big ship the 'Georgic'.

Mr. Ismay was not so absorbed in business as to neglect public matters. During the years 1877–78, when the Russo-Turkish was seemed likely to involve this country in hostilities, the White Star fleet was offered to the government for transport or cruisers; and out of this developed the arrangement by which the Government, by subsidy, secures the right to use certain first-class merchant steamers as war cruisers in the case of necessity. At the Spithead naval review of 1897, the White Star steamer 'Teutonic', armed as a cruiser with sixteen guns, was sent by Mr. Ismay to participate in the naval display, and show that mercantile cruisers were not myths. Even in 1889 the 'Teutonic' had participated in a naval review, and on that occasion she was inspected by the Prince of Wales and the German Emperor. The following year Mr. and Mrs. Ismay and several members of their family made a voyage round the world. Five years later fellow shareholders in the company presented Mr. Ismay with his portrait by Millias, and a service of plate. In 1888 Mr. and Mrs. Ismay travelled to the Far East. It was in 1892 that Mr. Ismay retired from the firm Ismay, Imrie and Co., though he retained the chairmanship of the White Star Company whose fleet then comprised 18 of 99,000 tons and 12 sailing vessels of 18,000 tons, but the aggregate in 1899 was increased to 164,000 tons. Mr. Ismay was also a director of the London and North-Western Railway Company and the Royal Insurance Company, and chairman of the Liverpool and London Steamship Protection Association. It is understood that it was Mr. Ismay's influence that caused the London and North-Western Railway Company to utilise the Waterloo Tunnel for passenger traffic from the riverside to Edgehill at Liverpool.

Though Mr. Ismay several times declined competing for parliamentary honours in Liverpool and elsewhere, he was recognised as a staunch Liberal Unionist, and performed useful public work in many directions. He was chairman of the Audit Commissioners of the Merseyside docks and Harbour Board, though he was never a member of the board or of the Liverpool City Council. As far back as 1884 he served on Lord Ravensworth's Admiralty Committee on the contract v dockyard systems building and repairing her Majesty's ships. Four years later he was on Lord Hartington's Royal Commission on Army and Navy Administration, while in the following year he was chairman of the Board of Trade Life Saving Appliances Committee. In 1891 he was on Admiral Tryon's Admiralty Committee on the naval reserve, as well as on the Royal Committee of Labour, and four years after he served on the Board of Trade Committee on side-lights. The Prince of Wales nominated Mr. Ismay to serve on the Royal British Commission of the Paris Exhibition 1900. It is understood that an offer of Royal recognition in the shape of a title was tendered to Mr. Ismay more than once, but that he declined such honours. Mr. Ismay was one of the founders of the training school Indefatigable and a liberal supporter of the Liverpool Seamen's Orphan Institution, while in 1887 he gave £20,000 towards a pension fund for worn-out Liverpool sailors, in celebration of the Queens Jubilee and his own 50th year. The fund is now doubled, and from it 100 sailors get £20 each year.

Mr. Ismay married in 1851 Margaret, daughter of the late Mr. Luke Bruce, ship owner, and the issue was three sons and four daughters. The sons are in the shipping business and one daughter is the wife of Mr. Geoffrey Drage, M.P. for Derby. One son, Mr. Joseph Bruce Ismay, married a daughter of Mr. George Schieffelin, of New York, and another son, James Hainsworth Ismay, married Margaret, eldest daughter of the 6th Marquis of Hertford. Mr. Ismay's residence was in Cheshire, of which he was a J.P. and D.L., and in 1892 he was High Sheriff. He was also J.P. for Lancashire. On July 20, 1899, he was made a Freeman of Belfast in circumstances which indicated how highly that city appreciated Mr. Ismay's share in contributing to its prosperity.[1]

Thomas' wife Margaret survived her husband by seven years, continuing to live at the Dawpool residence for just a short while following the death of her husband. The local school at Dawpool was situated very close to the Ismay's family home and was in a poor state of disrepair. The school being so small and now considered unfit for purpose, a decision was made in 1902 to build a new school close by. This was also the year which the White Star Line was absorbed into the International Mercantile Marine. Margaret donated £2,300 toward the cost of the new school, leaving a shortfall of £165.00, which was donated by residents of the parish. Work commenced on the new school in 1905, with Mrs Ismay being given the honour of laying the foundation stone and formally opening the school a year later. Soon after the new school was opened, Margaret felt she could no longer live in the mansion house and arranged to stay with her daughter Ethel, who, along with her husband Geoffrey Drage, had a large house in London. Following a short period of poor health, Margaret passed away in April 1907.

5

JOSEPH BRUCE ISMAY

The second child of Thomas and Margaret Ismay, Joseph Bruce, was born 12 December 1862 at Enfield House, Crosby, near Liverpool. He was preceded by a sister, Mary, two years his elder, and the first child of Thomas and Margaret. Bruce adored his sister, but this wonderful sibling love was to come to an early and sudden end when Mary contracted scarlet fever and died at 11 years of age.

It took many years for Bruce to come to terms with the loss of his dear sister and companion. The young Bruce was also trying to come to terms with the loss of his younger brother, Henry Sealby Ismay, whom the family had lost at just 2 years of age.

The following year, on 4 March 1867, Bruce's second brother James was born, followed three years later by another sister, Ethel. Soon afterwards, in January 1872, Margaret gave birth to the first of two sets of twins, Ada and Dora, followed by Charles Bower and Charlotte, just two years later.

Bruce was devoted to his parents, but Thomas found him difficult. He did not cope well with his father's strict discipline.

He had a difficult childhood, being caught between the loss of his much-loved siblings and his father's lack of understanding. One such example was a moment of youthful excitement.

Bruce had arrived home early, knowing that his father had been delayed in a meeting. It was a fine evening, and Bruce decided to take some exercise, so he took one of the horses for a gallop along the nearby sands of the River Dee. Unfortunately, he took his father's favourite racehorse. The horse stumbled heavily on the sand, broke a leg, and had to be destroyed. On his return home, Thomas became very angry with his son for taking the horse without his permission and for being so careless. Bruce was dreadfully upset about the incident and rarely rode a horse again.

The young Bruce began his schooling at New Brighton, some 10 miles from his home. It is most likely that he attended Somerville School, which was known as a 'preparatory school for the sons of gentlemen'. Interestingly, the building was at some point owned by Captain Henry Flinn, a founder of the Dominion Shipping Line, a steamship company that later amalgamated into the International Mercantile Marine Co. in 1902. Once his primary education at New Brighton was complete, Bruce was sent to Elstree, north London, and from there, to Harrow.

Bruce was similar in character to that of his mother, and like her, he was very shy and highly sensitive. This is likely to have resulted in an unhappy childhood throughout his school days. He began to show an abrupt, discourteous façade, perhaps hoping that this would prevent him from appearing over-sensitive, but his defensive façade often caused people to dislike him until they knew him well.

Bruce was very much devoted to his parents, and they loved him equally, but his father found him difficult in many ways. Thomas liked to consider a problem from every angle before he would reach a decision, whereas Bruce was quick thinking, and would state his opinion forcefully and without evasion.

After leaving Harrow, Bruce, now 16 years old, was sent to the north-western French town of Dinard, for private tuition to supplement his mainstream education. At that time, Dinard had recently become popular among the British and American social elite and was rapidly developing into one of the most popular resorts in Europe. During his residence at Dinard, Bruce became a highly skilled tennis player and enjoyed the sport for many years to come.

On 13 September 1880, at 18 years of age, Bruce began his apprenticeship at the head office of the White Star Line, Liverpool. His father always insisted that the young man should begin his career with no special privileges and should begin in the same manner as any other employee, and he was about to make his intentions clear. While attending school, Bruce had often accompanied his father to his office during the holidays; this was something which Thomas encouraged as he always hoped that his eldest son would one day succeed him as head of the White Star Line. On such occasions, Bruce would hang up his overcoat and hat in the office alongside his father's. When he began his first day as an employee, he did this as usual, but once he received his instructions and left the room, his father summoned a clerk and said to him, 'Please inform the new office boy that he is not to leave his hat and coat lying about in my office.' This simple instruction must have left the office staff with little doubt that the 'new office boy' would enter the company with very few special privileges, and also delivered the same message to Bruce, likely leaving him feeling humiliated in front of his father's staff. Perhaps this demonstrates a lack of understanding by Thomas towards his son and highlights the deep-rooted sense of inferiority which Bruce seemingly often felt.

After three years working for his father's company, Bruce, now 21 years of age, was nearing completion of his apprenticeship, so Thomas deemed that the time was right to send his eldest son on a voyage, to gain experience of the sea and of the world, just as Thomas had done when he was young.

When his two years overseas tour was over, Bruce returned home. He was 23 years old and had developed into a handsome young man. He stood 6ft 4in tall, he was slim, athletic and always immaculately dressed. Bruce was a keen tennis player and had become very good at it. During his recent tour of Australasia, he had played a great amount of tennis and was invited to umpire some of the matches in Australia. He had greatly enjoyed the adventure and benefited from experiencing differing customs and meeting many different people.

On Bruce's return to England, his father met him at the Albert Dock, Liverpool. His parents were delighted to see him home, especially as it was Christmas. This year there was to be a large party at their Dawpool home, and the whole family gathered for Christmas dinner. Bruce's stay was to be short as he was soon to depart for New York, where he was to take up a position in the White Star office. It was his parents' hope that he would eventually become New York's White Star agent.

Much to his parent's delight, he completed his training in February 1887. He almost immediately replaced existing White Star agent Mr R. Cortis, following his retirement, becoming the youngest agent to represent a major shipping company.

Bruce had finally escaped from his father's strict discipline and quickly began to live life to the full and by his own rules. He loved the social life that New York provided and was about to make the most of his freedom. While in New York he made many friends, one of whom was Harold Sanderson, future head of the White Star Line, and whose son Basil would one day marry Bruce's daughter, Evelyn.

Another member of his elite circle of friends was William Randolph Hearst. He had recently taken over his father's San Francisco newspaper and was keen to expand. Hearst invited Ismay to become a business partner, but Bruce had an intense dislike for newspapers, especially Hearst's style of the so-called 'yellow journalism' and so he declined the invitation. Hearst took Ismay's refusal very personally, resulting in a bitter conflict between them. It was a conflict that would later result in Hearst's newspapers launching a vicious attack on Bruce Ismay and the White Star Line following the *Titanic* disaster.

★★★

Meanwhile, back in England, his parents were hearing talk of Bruce's unruly behaviour and were becoming increasingly concerned, but their feelings of anxiety were about to become feelings of great joy. It was probably not by coincidence that Bruce was invited to spend the weekend at the home of a friend on Long Island. This was close to the home of Mrs Florence Beekman, younger sister of Bruce's future mother-in-law. It was during this visit that he met Miss Julia Florence Schieffelin, a beautiful young woman with a bright and joyful disposition.

Florence was the eldest daughter of Mr and Mrs George Richard Schieffelin, one of the most respected families in New York society, and she was known in society life as 'the Belle of New York'. Bruce adored her, and afterwards would watch out for her each afternoon as she passed the window of his apartment, located on the corner of West 42nd Street and Fifth Avenue. On his first meeting with her, Bruce had not made a good impression, as she saw only the ostentation of his boyish behaviour. Despite her initial trepidation, they met on several occasions afterwards, and the attraction between them began to flourish.

The following Thanksgiving, Mrs Beekman held a party at New Jersey's Tuxedo Club, at which Bruce and Florence were among the many invited guests. Bruce had left his former life behind, and all his thoughts were of her. Early in the evening, Bruce invited Florence to accompany him on a walk by the lake, where she agreed to marry him.

Her father was quite apprehensive about the proposal. It was not that he disliked Bruce, indeed the contrary was true, but he loved his daughter very much, and as she was only 18 years of age, he considered her too young for marriage. He also feared that Bruce would take his daughter to live in England and so he told them that they must wait a while until they became surer of themselves.

Meanwhile, Bruce had received similar advice from his parents, so the couple reluctantly agreed to hold their plans for one year. Florence's parents could see that the young couple deeply loved one another, and in April the following year, her father agreed to the announcement of their engagement but stipulated one condition. Bruce had to make a promise to Florence's parents that they would continue to live in America, a promise that Bruce was happy to give. Subsequently, the young couple became officially engaged on 7 April 1888. It was probably no coincidence that this date was also the wedding anniversary of Bruce's parents. Their engagement was reported by *New York 'Truth'* on 12 April:

Miss Florence Schieffelin, whose engagement with Mr. J. Bruce Ismay has just been announced, is a charming girl with real brown hair, beautiful eyes and a singularly winsome manner. She has been an undisputed belle during her two seasons and a number of swells, who grow on our native heath feel desolated that an Englishman, be he never so desirable, should have won such a genuine prize. Miss Schieffelin is the daughter of Mr. George R. Schieffelin. Her mother was a Miss Delaplaine, a name that is a guarantee for beauty, brains, birth and worth. She is a niece of that gracious and graceful woman, Mrs. James Hude Beekman.

On 4 December of that year, the couple were married at the Church of the Heavenly Rest in New York, with their marriage being reported by several leading newspapers:

A brilliant and fashionable assemblage gathered at noon yesterday in the Church of the Heavenly Rest, on Fifth-Avenue, to witness the marriage of Miss Florence Schieffelin, a daughter of George R. Schieffelin and a great favourite in New-York society, and Mr. J. Bruce Ismay, the Agent of the White Star Steamship Line. Mr Schieffelin and his family are members of Grace Church but selected the Church of the Heavenly Rest for the ceremony on account of its proximity to their residence on Forty-fifth-street. The Rev. Dr. Huntington of Grace Church, assisted by the Rev. D. Parker Morgan, the Rector of the Church of the Heavenly Rest, were the officiating clergymen.

The bride wore a gown of white brocade richly trimmed with old point lace. A veil of old point also fell over her face, confined by a tiara of diamonds. A diamond pendant hanging from a necklace of pearls sparkled at her throat.

She carried a large bouquet of lilies of the valley. Preceding her were the two little maids of honor, her sisters, Miss Sadie and Miss Constance Schieffelin, who wore white silk dresses, white hats, and carried baskets of pink roses. The ushers were Messrs. Bond Emerson, T.J. Oakley Rhinelander, Amory Sibley Carhart, Edward Perry, and Fleming Crooks of England. The groom's best man was Mr. Ernest Bliss.

At the conclusion of the ceremony a wedding break-fast was given to the young couple along with their close friends at the residence of the bride's father, 8, East Forty-Fifth-Street. Among those present were Mr. John Jay, Mrs. Ernest Crosby, Mr. and Mrs. James Beekman, Mr. and Mrs. William Rhinelander, Mr. and Mrs. Philip Rhinelander, Mr. and Mrs. William Schieffelin, The Misses Rhinelander, Miss Fannie Walker, the Misses Webb, Mrs. W. S. Livingston, Miss Eleanor Robinson, Mrs. Eastman Johnson, Miss Johnson, and Miss Marie Van Deuser Reed.[1]

For reasons which remain unknown, Thomas and Margaret did not travel to New York to witness Bruce and Florence's marriage, but a clue may be found in Margaret's diary, where she writes about what is likely to have been a very important dinner with Mr Cunard and Mr John Burns, both being senior figures within the Cunard Line. The dinner took place just a few days before Bruce and Florence's wedding, which would have left them little time to make the crossing to New York. Margaret later wrote of the wedding in her diary:

November 28th, Wednesday, 1888.
Mr. & Mrs. Burns and their two daughters & Mr. Cunard dined with us at the Salisbury.

December 4th, Tuesday, 1888.
    Bruce and Florence Schieffelin are married today at the Church of Heavenly Rest, New York, may God's best blessing rest on them.

Bruce and his bride honeymooned at Philadelphia's Lafayette Hotel, returning to New York one week later. On arrival in New York, the newlyweds boarded the White Star liner *Adriatic*, bound for Liverpool, as Bruce was keen to take his wife to England to spend Christmas with his family at his parent's Dawpool home.

They arrived at the Albert Dock, Liverpool, on the morning of 22 December and were greeted there by Bruce's father, Thomas. Margaret Ismay records the excitement of their arrival in her diary:

> December 22nd, Saturday, 1888. T.H.I. went in early and went on board Adriatic to meet Bruce and Florence after which they drove out, bells ringing. Supper night to over 100 got up by Jimmy, fireworks and a large bonfire – they met with a hearty welcome from all.

Naturally, the Ismay family were eager to welcome Florence into their home, and they immediately loved her, especially Bruce's younger sister, Ethel, now 18 years old and twins Ada and Dora, now 16. The young ladies were intrigued by her soft New York accent, her style of dress and her lack of formality – a formality which they had all become accustomed to.

Florence had given them a window into another way of life, one other than that which was expected of a young lady growing up in upper-class Victorian England. Life in Dawpool, as with many other Victorian country homes, was very strict. It was not considered proper for a young lady to read a newspaper or to speak at the dinner table unless father spoke first.

Florence had been raised in a society that was much less inhibited than that of Victorian England. During her first meal at Dawpool, she chatted happily and unreservedly throughout dinner, much to the astonishment of Thomas and to the admiration of her sisters-in-law. The young ladies were charmed by her, and at the end of the evening, they all left for the new bride's bedroom where they were shown Florence's beautiful bridal gown, as they listened to her account of how she first met their charming brother.

Florence recorded her first visit to the Dawpool mansion. It is clear that the north-west of England, and Dawpool, provided a climate that she had not yet become accustomed to, 'It was bitterly cold, as the house had no central heating. The fires were not lit in the bedrooms until after tea. Every night before bed I heaped coal onto the fire, in the hope that it would last until morning; but it never did.'

Dawpool was a large mansion house but had a small number of bathrooms by comparison. It was necessary to have a bath and large jugs of hot water brought into Florence's bedroom, known as the Oak Room. Along with other family members and staff, Florence would rise from her bed at 6.30 each morning to join Thomas for family prayers at 7.30, after which Thomas would leave for Liverpool at exactly 8 o'clock.

The arrival of Bruce and his beautiful bride had been clouded to an extent by the death of Hannah Imrie, the wife of William Imrie, business partner and long-time friend of Thomas. A reception and ball had been arranged to celebrate the newlyweds' arrival at Dawpool. Mrs Imrie had expressed a particular wish to meet Florence, but the ball was cancelled out of respect for the grieving Mr Imrie and for his late wife.

This was Thomas and Margaret's fourth Christmas at Dawpool, and this time of the year was always looked forward to as a time for celebration with family and friends. This was, of course, a very special year, with the presence of their beautiful daughter-in-law, although the celebrations were somewhat marred by the loss of their good friend.

Bruce's bride wished to visit Ireland, so on the afternoon of 15 January, the newlyweds travelled to Belfast where they were met by a chauffeur, then on to Glenfarne Hall, the home of Sir Edward Harland and his wife, Rosa. Glenfarne Hall was a large mansion house in County Leitrim, Ireland. The mansion stood near the shores of Lough MacNean, where Bruce spent much of his time pursuing his hobbies, shooting and fishing, which he very much enjoyed. After an enjoyable week in Ireland, Bruce and Florence returned to Dawpool, where they stayed the night.

Another of Thomas Ismay's business partners, William Graves, along with his wife, was also anxious to meet Florence, so the following day, the newlyweds travelled to Mr and Mrs Graves' Dowsefield home. Mrs Graves had requested that Florence wear her wedding gown and shoes, but the weather being so cold, her feet had become very swollen, and consequently, she could only wear a pair of bedroom slippers. Thus, much to the surprise of Mr and Mrs Graves, Florence arrived at the dinner party wearing her exquisite bridal gown and her favourite slippers!

The following day, the newlyweds returned to Dawpool, before taking a previously arranged shopping trip to London. Margaret Ismay recalls in her diary:

January 28th, Monday 1889. On my return found Florence and Bruce here. Florence's feet are so bad with chilblains the Doctor forbid her going to London.

The following Thursday, the newlyweds journeyed to the Metropole Hotel, London, to be joined one week later by Bruce's mother and, soon afterwards, Thomas. The family thoroughly enjoyed their stay in the capital, during which time they found time to dine with several friends and visited many shops and theatres including the Lyceum, while Thomas, being ever diligent, also used the trip to take care of some pressing business matters, before returning to Liverpool several days later, so that Bruce and Florence could say goodbye to family and friends before returning to New York. Margaret Ismay records the trip in her diary thus:

> February 6th, Wednesday 1889. Peaker and I left by the 11 train for London, Arrived Euston 3.30. She took luggage to Metropole and I went to Madame Mansey to get dress altered. I joined Bruce and Florence at the Metropole and got a nice bed and dressing room, No. 301. Thomas came up by the 2 train and signed a number of bills L & NW [railway]. After dinner Bruce and Florence dining at Mrs. Rae's. Ethel went to stay at the Manor House.

> February 7th, Thursday 1889. Went with Bruce and Florence to several shops to look at furniture, bought some at Clarks and ordered dining room chairs etc. from Mr. Heaton. Mr. and Mrs. Pollock dined with us. I went afterwards to the Lyceum Theatre to watch Macbeth.

> February 8th, Friday 1886. Florence and I went to see The Academy and Grosvenor. Lunched at the Metropole, met Thomas and Mr. Heaton where we saw Mr. Rhodes, then I called upon Mrs. Dugdale and Mrs. Shwarbe. After dinner I went to The Criterion and saw Still Waters Run Deep. Thomas dining at Canon St. Hotel with Life Saving Appliances Committee.

> February 9th, Saturday 1889. Thomas travelled home by the 10 train as he wanted an hour at the office. Florence, Bruce and myself came down by the 12 train.

Bruce and Florence departed for New York aboard the White Star liner *Germanic* on 20 February, arriving eight days later, and instantly rented a house on Madison Avenue, New York.

In August of the same year, Thomas and Margaret decided to take a trip to New York, taking their children Ethel, Dora, Ada, Charles and Charlotte with them. They travelled on board RMS *Teutonic* for her maiden voyage, the passage taking almost eight days due to the bad weather they encountered during the crossing. Also on board were Lord William James Pirrie and his wife Margaret, daughter of John Carlisle. The Carlisles were also on board. The Honourable Alexander Carlisle was the chief designer for Harland & Wolff and was later to become the chief designer of *Olympic* and *Titanic*. Margaret Ismay records her experiences of *Teutonic's* maiden voyage:

August 7th, Wednesday. 1889. Left Dawpool at 2.30 p.m. to go on board the Teutonic at 4 p.m. rather a windy day. Mr. Imrie and Mr. Graves came to see us off with several friends.

August 8th, Thursday, Found some nice people on board, Sir Henry and Lady Lock and family, Lady Shrewsbury, Lady Selkirk, Sir Lyon and Lady Playfair. Arrived at Queenstown at 10.30 a.m. and left at 2 p.m. after taking mails aboard.

August 9th, Friday, 1889. Rather a bad night, also stormy this morning, although we all went into the Saloon for breakfast. It got worse during the afternoon, and one after another succumbed. A high wind, and a nasty sea, which made the Teutonic pitch.

August 10th, Saturday. The wind and sea very high, none of us got up for breakfast. But during the day some of us got up on deck. About 10 o'clock the sea came right on board, and took Sir Henry Lock right off his feet. Fortunately he was not hurt.

August 11th, Sunday. None of us able to go to Service except Thomas, but got up and went on deck in the afternoon.

August 12th, Monday. The sea and wind have gone down, but now we have a dense fog.

August 13th, Tuesday. Still very foggy, but had a concert, which would have been a failure, but for Mr. York. Thomas was in the Chair, and made some remarks which amused the audience. A collection was made, and £28 got for the Seamen's Orphanage.

August 14th, Wednesday. It appears that Thomas' remarks have given offence to some people on board, although unintended by him. In fact what they say is both unfair and untrue. Made the land late at night; reaching Sandy Hook just after midnight. Passage 6 days, 14 hours, 20 minutes.

August 15th, Thursday. Bruce came on board about 5 a.m. looking very ill and thin. Florence was on the wharf when we arrived and we landed about 11 a.m. Thomas, Dora, Lottie and myself went to the Windsor Hotel, Ethel, Ada and [Charles] Bower to Bruce's. We all dined with Bruce and Florence.

Thomas and Margaret had never met Florence's parents, so a dinner party was arranged at the home of Mr and Mrs Schieffelin. During their stay with the Schieffelin family, Bruce's youngest brother, Charles Bower, met Matilda Constance, the youngest sister of Florence. Constance, as she was always known, would later become his wife, much to the delight of Florence. Six days later, the Ismay family boarded *Teutonic* again for their return to England.

During Christmas of the same year, Thomas and Margaret were thrilled to receive news that their first grandchild had been born, a beautiful girl, to be named Margaret Bruce Ismay. To celebrate the news, Thomas and Margaret held a dance at Dawpool with 240 friends and family in attendance.

★★★

In July of 1890, Bruce, along with his wife and daughter, came to Dawpool for a visit. While they were there, Thomas suggested to Bruce that he, along with his younger brother James, should become partners of the firm of Ismay, Imrie & Co. He also asserted to Bruce that his wish was that he would follow him as head of the firm, but on condition that he and his family should return to England permanently. It was made clear to Bruce that if he did not agree to this condition, his younger brother James would be offered control of the company.

This placed Bruce in a very difficult situation. The couple were very happy in New York, and Bruce loved his position as agent for the White Star Line. He also remembered the promise he had given to Florence's parents, never to take their daughter to live outside of America. After much deliberation and to his father's disappointment, Bruce decided that he would uphold his promise to Mr George Schieffelin and return to America.

On their return, Mr and Mrs Schieffelin soon became aware of Thomas' suggestion and asked Bruce and Florence to join them for dinner, where they discussed the matter. Mr Schieffelin's advice to his daughter was that they should allow Bruce to withdraw from his earlier promise, as he had observed that Bruce was a highly ambitious man, and although there was little doubt that Bruce was currently happy with his life, he would likely resent the fact that his younger brother was head of Ismay, Imrie & Co. and possibly hold it against the Schieffelin family. Consequently, Bruce informed his father that they now planned to return to England to find a permanent home there.

On the first day of January 1891, Margaret records the following in her diary:

> January 1st, Thursday, 1891. Bruce and Jimmy admitted as partners to the Firm. I pray that they may be guided to do what is right, and have the integrity of their father.

On 3 April the same year, while still living in Maddson Avenue, New York, Florence gave birth to their first son, Henry Bruce, who would be followed three years later by another son, Thomas Bruce, known simply as Tom.

By August 1891, plans were well underway for the return of Bruce and his family, but although Thomas wished to have them all in England, he was not so happy at the thought of them at Dawpool for an extended period. He quickly found a property at Mossley Hill, Liverpool, which was considered suitable for their needs. It was also arranged that one of Thomas' house staff would be sent to cook for the family, so all would be ready for their arrival.

During this time, Bruce and Florence's son, Henry Bruce, now five months old, was not well. Knowing that they were about to leave for England, the family doctor felt that the sea trip would aid the baby's recovery. Unfortunately, the doctor had not fully realised the seriousness of the illness. Florence was not a good traveller at sea, and consequently, she was confined to her bunk during the whole journey, and therefore the young baby Henry was being cared for by a young Irish maid who was unable to give him the care that he needed. On their arrival at Liverpool docks, they were met by Thomas and James, who were shocked to see the condition of the baby. Thomas said, 'That baby is going to die; he must see a doctor immediately.'

Margaret describes this, and the following days in her diary, with great sadness:

> September 30th, Wednesday, 1891. Thomas and Jimmy drove in to meet Bruce and telephoned us to say that the baby was very poorly and that he had telephoned for Dr. Russell. They got home at 10.30 a.m., and I was shocked to see the little thing looking so ill. Dr Russell thought badly of him. In the evening the baby got so much worse that we sent for Dr. Russell again, and he remained the night.

> October 1st, Thursday. The baby no better, seems weaker to me. Dr. Russell left at 8 a.m. and returned at 11.30 a.m. Gave him brandy and beef tea, at 3 p.m. he became much worse and at 4 p.m. he passed away. We are sadly grieved about it.

> October 2nd, Friday. Thomas in the house all day, in great distress, and very sorry that Bruce and Florence should have such a sad homecoming.

> October 3rd, Saturday. Mr. Jackson's carriage with the body, Thomas Bruce and Jimmy left here at 9.45 a.m. for Anfield Cemetery, where the little baby was laid, they got back here about 3 p.m.

The tragic loss of his eldest son was something that Bruce could not come to terms with, and for a great many years afterwards he had a tendency to avoid children. Years later, he even went to the extreme of having an additional wing built onto his future home, Sandheys, the main purpose of which was to accommodate the children separately, the only exception being his eldest daughter Margaret, who always held a special place in his heart.

★★★

However, Bruce was about to take on another huge responsibility. On 21 December 1891, Thomas informed Bruce, along with his brother James, that it was his intention to retire from the firm of Ismay, Imrie & Co. on 1 January the following year. This would necessitate Bruce taking on much more responsibility within the company. Eight days after hearing this announcement, Bruce, Florence and their daughter Margaret moved into their new home, Wiston House on Mossley Hill Road. Florence was unimpressed with the house, but for now, it was to be their new home.

Her first years in England were far from happy, living in a house which she very much disliked, she had lost her first son, and perhaps wondered how different life would be if they had not made the crossing to live in England. In New York, she was very well known and equally well liked. Florence had come to live in northern England during winter, she knew very few people, and due to his business commitments, her husband was out of the house all day and often for several days at a time.

Florence was devoted to her younger sister, Constance, and had asked her to visit. She gladly accepted the invitation and came to live with them for some considerable time. Constance and Bruce's younger brother, Bower, saw much of one another, and a special attraction began to flourish.

Five months after moving into Wiston House, Bruce and Florence found Sandheys was for sale. Sandheys was a large Georgian-style house, standing in 10 acres of ground and located close to their present rented accommodation. The couple loved the fine building and were determined to finalise the purchase and move in as quickly as possible.

★★★

Eight years later, Florence was delighted to learn that another wedding was about to take place. Constance was to marry Charles Bower. Bruce's mother was not happy at the thought of her youngest son entering into marriage, as she felt that they were both too young and it was too soon after the recent tragic loss of his father. As can be seen from Margaret's diary, the young Bower and Constance had their wish:

January 10th, Wednesday, 1900. Mr. Schieffelin and Constance arrived at Southampton, Ada and Dora went there to meet them. They dined here. [Dawpool]

January 11th, Thursday, 1900. Mr Schieffelin came to tea. Ada and Dora dined with the Schieffelins. Florence and Bower came to town.

January 12th, Friday, 1900. Mr. Schieffelin told me that he thought it best for Bower and Constance to be married before he went away. I was very surprised and said that I could not agree with him, and that I felt strongly that they better wait until he returned. Found however that he was quite determined it should be. Bower had already applied for a special licence.

January 13th, Saturday, 1900. Bower married to Constance Schieffelin at St. Pauls, Knightsbridge by Mr. Villiers. I did not go to the church as I did not feel equal to it, Ethel stayed with me.

January 14th, Sunday, 1900. Ethel and I went to church; Bower and Constance came to say goodbye, as they are leaving for Newcastle. Mr. Schieffelin left for Liverpool.

After the wedding, life at Dawpool was never the same. Bruce Ismay found that he was required to spend increasingly more time away from England's shores. His younger brother James, also a partner in their father's firm, was beginning to show less interest in shipping, turning his attention to farming, retiring from the family business two years later, along with William Imrie and William Samuel Graves, leaving Bruce and Harold Sanderson in sole charge of the company. Keeping an interest in these changes was American businessman John Pierpont Morgan, whose ambition was to monopolise the shipping trade. Morgan was slowly making his plans to buy majority shares of the Oceanic Steam Navigation Company, parent company of the White Star Line.

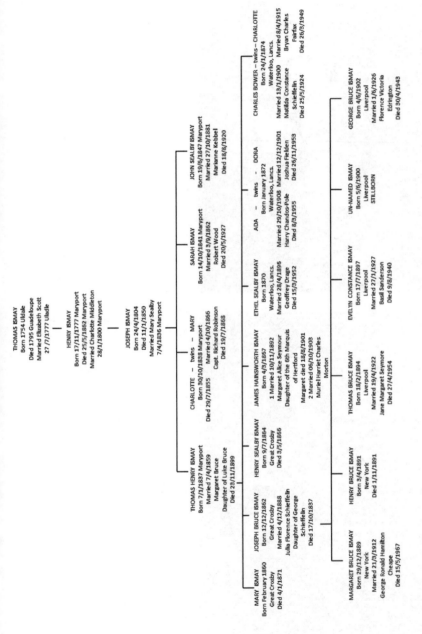

Bruce Ismay's family tree.

Thomas Henry Ismay, aged about 21 years.

T.H. Ismay painting by Herkomer.

Mrs T.H. Ismay, aged about 56 years.

T.H. Ismay receiving the Freedom of Belfast, 1899. Back row (left–right):
Lady Margaret Ismay, James Ismay, Dora Ismay, J. Bruce Ismay, Thomas Henry
Ismay, Mrs Bruce Ismay, Geoffrey Drage. Front row: Charles Ismay, Ethel Drage,
Mrs T.H. Ismay, Ada Ismay, Charlotte (Lottie) Ismay.

William Imrie, partner of Ismay, Imrie & Co.

White Star Line head office, Liverpool. (Courtesy of Jonathon Wild)

White Star Line's first class ticket office, Liverpool. (Courtesy of Jonathon Wild)

White Star Line's first class ticket office, Liverpool. (Courtesy of Jonathon Wild)

Bruce Ismay as a young boy.

Bruce Ismay, around the time he married Florence Schieffelin.

The New York home of Bruce Ismay, on the corner of 5th Avenue and West 42nd Street.

The bedroom of Bruce's apartment.

Julia Florence Ismay.

Bruce Ismay around the time when he took the chairmanship of the White Star Line.

Margaret Bruce Ismay, eldest child of Bruce and Florence.

Thomas Bruce Ismay, second son of Bruce and Florence.

Constance Schieffelin, sister of Florence.

Sandheys, Liverpool. The home of Bruce and Florence from 1893–1920.

Sandheys' lounge.

Sandheys' reception room.

Cedric leaving New York with Bruce Ismay on board after accepting the presidency of IMM.

HMS *Conway*.

6

PRESIDENCY OF INTERNATIONAL MERCANTILE MARINE

Following his father's death, Bruce Ismay took the helm of the White Star Line, closely supported by his brother James and his father's close friends, William Imrie and William Graves, all being business partners. Although Bruce's skills differed from that of his father, the ethos of the company would, for now, remain unchanged.

As a child, Bruce was shy and exceedingly sensitive, which continued into his adult life. Those who did not know him well found him to be arrogant and impatient. He was highly critical, and many of his staff felt threatened by him. If asked his opinion, he would give it quickly and forthrightly, without accepting any argument to the contrary. Much of this was due to his defensive façade, which he, likely unconsciously, built up to hide his shy sensitivity.

Bruce always insisted on punctuality, especially within the office, something he inherited from his father. His office staff were very much aware of this, and on arriving for an appointment with him, they would stand outside the office door, waiting to knock at the exact appointed time.

Bruce disliked any contact with the press and consequently became unpopular with them. If a reporter approached him directly, he would usually remind them that the White Star Line had a helpful publicity department. He was incapable of speaking in public and could never make a speech to a large audience. His lack of self-expression, together with his unpopularity with the press, would later haunt him.

There were those who understood Bruce well and had gained his confidence. They saw another side to him – a kind and generous man, of good character and trustworthy. Unlike his father, Bruce was very quick thinking. He would often find the answer to a problem almost immediately, but on those occasions when an answer was not immediately obvious, he would walk from his home to the office, a distance of 3 quiet miles. By the time he reached the office, he would usually have found the solution.

On one such occasion, Bruce chanced upon some children playing on a roof. Once he arrived at work, he sent for one of his trusted staff and described the building with its flat roof, quickly being informed that it was an orphanage. Bruce quickly instructed his office to make out a cheque for £500 and immediately sent it to the orphanage.

One year after Bruce was made chairman of the company, *Celtic* was launched at Belfast. This was a meaningful and emotional time for the family, as this was the last ship ordered before his father's death. Margaret made the following entry in her diary:

April 4th, Thursday, 1901. The Celtic successfully launched. This is the last order my dearest one gave to Messrs. Harland

& Wolff. She is the largest ship in the world. Bruce unable to be present, as little Evelyn is very ill with diphtheria.

It could be said that the launch of *Celtic* marked a further stage in their policy of building large ships capable of carrying a great number of passengers, along with a large cargo. In the year that *Celtic* was launched, the shipping trade was in depression, partly due to a large reduction in the number of emigrants travelling to America and partly also to the vicious rates war between several shipping companies.

It was perhaps no coincidence that the wealthy American financier John Pierpont Morgan deemed the time right to make his move into the shipping world. Until 1901, Morgan's business interests lay mainly with merging the American Railroads, and he now planned to do similar with steamship companies. His plan was to buy up various companies and form a combine, the ultimate goal being to eliminate the rates war. At that time, the Americans had few ships of their own working the Atlantic trade. The British Inman Line was absorbed into the American Line in 1893, and, although the line was now American-owned, US law dictated that no ship could fly the US flag unless it was built in that country.

Pierpont Morgan began with the purchase of the Red Star Line, quickly followed by the American Line, Atlantic Transport Line and soon afterwards he acquired the Dominion Line. On 1 October 1902, Morgan, along with Clement Griscom, former head of the American Line and the Red Star Line, announced the founding of the International Mercantile Marine Company (IMM).

In the same year, Morgan approached the White Star Line offering to pay the shareholders ten times the value of the line's income for the year ending 1900. That year had proved to be a particularly successful one for White Star, therefore the shareholders would make a considerable profit. It was also proposed that Bruce would retain his position as chairman of the line and other senior partners, William Imrie, William Graves and James Ismay would retire; only Bruce's close friend, Harold Sanderson would remain.

Although Bruce consulted heavily with his family and other shareholders, he was placed in a difficult position. His father, Thomas, had been a millionaire, but when his estate was divided, Bruce's share was £100,000, kept in trust. Therefore, unlike his father, he did not have large resources to rely on, but he felt that if he could retain his position of chairman of the White Star Line, he would still maintain a degree of control over the company.

One instruction in Thomas' will was in relation to his daughters. He had stipulated that none of his daughters should invest capital into any other shipping company, therefore, they were unable to exert any influence in these matters. Eventually, 75 per cent of shareholders decided to accept Morgan's offer, and so all parties were forced to accept, and the sale was completed in December 1902.

Margaret Ismay recorded her feelings in her diary:

December 1st, Monday. Messrs Morgan have paid all the Shareholders of the Oceanic Steam Navigation Company for their shares. This ends the White Star Line in which so much interest, thought and care was bestowed and which was my dearest one's life's work. Bruce continues with the firm as Manager.

After only one year of trading, the IMM found itself in an uncertain financial position, with the current president, Clement Griscom, in poor health and nearing retirement. As the White Star Line was now part of Morgan's IMM combine, and Bruce was currently managing director and chairman of the White Star Line, Morgan felt that Bruce would be the ideal man to replace Griscom as president of the IMM. Accordingly, Morgan, along with his associates, approached Bruce with a view to replacing Griscom as president of the company.

The idea did not appeal to Bruce, as he felt that the position would interfere too much with his private life. He was happy in England, but the head office of the IMM was in America. He also thought that this position would attract a great deal of publicity – something which he intensely disliked – although such publicity would seem small in comparison to that he would receive over eight years later with the sinking of *Titanic*.

Mr Griscom, Mr Charles Steele, Lord Pirrie and Sir Clinton Dawkins all attempted to impress on Bruce that he was the ideal person to take on this position, as did Mr Albert Ballin of the Hamburg-America Line. On 24 December 1903, Ballin wrote a confidential letter to Bruce, the purpose of which was to convey his concerns regarding the current manager of the IMM, Mr Clement Griscom, and also to encourage Bruce to accept presidency of the IMM:

Hamburg, December 24th 1903

My dear Mr Ismay,

I just received your kind telegram and I need not assure you that I reciprocate your good wishes most sincerely for you personally and for the White Star line.

I have been very busy owing to my engagements at Cologne; I could not wait at London to meet you. I wanted so very much to talk to you about the combine, which has been quite a great disappointment to me as it probably was to you so far.

You know I advocated the scheme here with much enthu-siasm, and I am still convinced that the plan was alright and that they were simply wrong in the way in which they put this combination on its legs.

I told (as I may mention secretly to you) Mr Morgan that it did not only require a big man to make such combine, but that it requires quite so big a man to steer it and that he asked my advice and recalled when he appointed Clement Griscom to be the President.

Well, I hope when you come over you will find our friends very reasonable and I further hope most sincerely that you will take the whole combine under your wings. I should be only too glad if you did, and I trust you could make it a success. Please consider this letter quite confidential.

With all good wishes believe me dear Mr Ismay

Sincerely yours,

[signed] Ballin

By the beginning of 1904, the offer of presidency of the IMM was beginning to appeal to Bruce and in January of that year he sailed for New York, accompanied by his wife Florence, so that he could discuss the matter in more detail. While in New York, he sent the following correspondence to Harold Sanderson:

Holland House, New York
February 7th, 1904

My Dear Harold,

Thinking you might like to know what was going on, I sent you the following cable on Saturday:-

'Griscom very cordial, most anxious should accept position. Steele laid up, arranged conference Monday.'

I was met on arrival by Griscom, his son and Jim Wright. Griscom came on board, and told me he wished to have a talk with me before I saw anyone else, so went up to his rooms at 10 o'clock on Friday morning, and had two hours talk with him.

He was very friendly and cordial, and I am extremely sorry to say I find him much altered for the worse since I was last here, and fear he is in a most indifferent state of health.

He told me his object in seeing me was to ask me to take the position of president, as he felt strongly the power and control should be in Liverpool, and that I was the proper and only person fit to undertake and carry on the business in a satisfactory manner, and he assured me I could count on the loyal co-operation and hearty assistance of himself, his son, and Wilding, in fact, of all the people on this side. I told him I was sorry he had decided to resign from the presidency, and fully appreciated his kind references to myself, and also his wish that I should assume the office of president; but that before I could arrive at any decision in regard thereto, I would require to have the fullest information in reference to the financial position of the company, as I felt it would be absolutely impossible to hope to achieve any measure of success if we were to be constantly hampered by lack of funds. In this he quite agreed, and was in accord with my views that unless money was forthcoming, it would be foolish of me to undertake the responsibility of managing the I.M.M. Company, and promised to support me to get the situation cleared up when we have the meeting with Steele and Morgan.

I asked him whether, in his opinion, it was possible to make the I.M.M. Company a commercial success, and to this question he replied in the affirmative, adding that if he was younger and in a better state of health, there is nothing he would like more than to undertake the work, but that it would be essential that money should be at his command, for he well knew from his own experience during the last twenty years what it meant to be hampered for lack of funds. He also agreed that it is necessary the Leyland Line position should be defined, as at present the situation was an impossible one. We also touched on a great many matters of detail, but nothing transpired which affected the main point.

I came down town with him, and went to the office, where I found a telephone message from Steele, advising me he was laid up at home with a cold, and would not be down town.

Morgan is off on a jaunt in Canada, but fancy he returns to the city today, so hope to arrange a meeting of Morgan, Steele, Griscom and myself early this week when I hope the whole matter may be frankly and fully discussed.

Another letter followed two days later:

Holland House, New York
February 9th, 1904

I saw Steele yesterday for about an hour. He is better, but still far from well. After a little general conversation, I asked him what was the position of affairs here, and he told me 'Bad, and most unsatisfactory'. I asked what he proposed doing about it, and he replied by saying I was the one to deal with the situation, and that they wanted me to undertake the presidency and assume full and absolute control. I replied that before I could even seriously consider the suggestion, I must know what was the financial position of the company. He told me it was bad. I then said, 'I suppose J. P. Morgan & Company are prepared to put their hands in their pocket, and help the I.M.M. Company?' He said he did not know about that then I said, 'if you cannot see your way to stand behind the I.M.M.

Company, you might as well put up the shutters at once' to which he answered, 'Well, I suppose we must see it through; at the same time, we have already between $2,000,000 and $3,000,000 invested in it.'

He then gave me a lot of figures, which I glanced through last night, but have not mastered, showing how the $5,000,000 has been disposed of, and sundry other information, which I intend going through today with Swartz, if possible.

We got on to the position of the Leyland Line, which is one that must be dealt with. I cannot do better, or explain the position to you more fully, than by asking you to request Wilding to show you the copies of all cables that have passed between him and the people here. The position is a ludicrous and impossible one, and must be straightened out. Steele is most annoyed about it.

I am writing you at the hotel and am just off to meet Morgan, Steele and Griscom at the former's house, so shall doubtless be in a position to cable you this afternoon the result of my interview. It is a difficult proposition, and I intend going slow, and giving the matter the most earnest and careful consideration. It is easy to jump in, but it would be difficult, if not impossible, to climb out.

yours sincerely,

[Signed] J. Bruce Ismay

Holland House, New York

Later the same day, Bruce met with Morgan, Steele and Griscom as arranged. Once the meeting was over, he sent the following message to Harold Sanderson, highlighting the main points discussed:

Tuesday, February 9th, 1904.

My dear Harold, I sent you the following cable this afternoon, viz.:-

Had meeting Morgan, Steele, Griscom present, offered me presidency and unlimited control. Morgan thinks my residing here portion each year absolutely necessary. This entirely new proposition. He does not consider my nationality any drawback, but possibly advantageous. Accepting proposal would involve dividing my time between England and America, and giving up all outside interests. Expect in time my stay in America would be comparatively short. He expressed his views most strongly, and very anxious I should accept. Have told him will give proposal consideration. Most difficult know what to do; please cable your views and mother's fully. Am very anxious and curious to receive your reply. And also to have my mother's views thereon, and hope you have been able to go over to Dawpool and discuss the matter with her.

As arranged, I went to Morgan's house this morning, and there met Morgan, Steele and Griscom, and we had a discussion on the whole situation.

Morgan was extremely cordial and pleasant, and opened out by saying he was extremely dissatisfied with the present position of affairs, and felt the whole organisation was on wrong lines. He stated he did not mind losing money, but he did object to doing so owing to poor organisation. He felt things were on a wrong basis, and that, in his opinion, I was the only man he knew that could straighten matters out. He was prepared to make me president and give me unlimited control, and anything I decided was to be final, and he was tired of all the cabling that was going on between America and England, and wanted to feel there was some individual who was absolutely responsible for the working of the I.M.M. Co.

He further stated in his opinion it was essential that if I accepted the proposal he made that I should take a house in New York, and spend a certain portion of the year here, it might be four or six months, but of that I would be the best judge.

In regard to finances he stated his feeling was that the earnings of the subsidiary companies should be allocated to paying the fixed charges, any surplus over and above this should go to pay Pirrie, and was willing this [Pirrie's indebtedness] should be a prior charge on the company to any indebtedness to his firm. In the event of the company not earning sufficient to pay the fixed charges he was himself prepared to make any deficiency good for three years. I told him I considered nothing could be fairer than this, and he replied, 'Could any man say more', to which I said 'No.'

After he had got through I said that no one was more anxious to make the I.M.M. Co. a success than I was, but referred to a conversation I had had with him seven months ago, when the question of an Englishman being the president of the company was discussed, and that he then stated he felt it was not possible. To this he replied that he had no recollection of the incident, but now felt strongly that instead of this being a drawback, it would be an advantage, as it would let the public see that they intended to do all they knew to make the I.M.M. Co. a commercial success.

I next stated the proposition in regard to my living in New York was an entirely new one, and that I did not like the idea. He replied that in view of the company being an American one, it was necessary I should, as president, have a domicile here, and that it was for me to decide how much of my time it was necessary to spend here, recognising the fact that the business must be controlled and emanate in England.

We had a good deal of general conversation, the interview lasting the best part of two hours, and ending by my saying I would carefully consider the matter.

There is no doubt Morgan, Steele and Griscom are really anxious I should take the position, but I do not like the idea of living here, even for a period of each year; it would mean my giving up all my outside interests, the L. & N.W. [London and Northern Railway], Globe, Sea and other companies in which I take an interest. On the other hand, it is an opportunity of pulling together a concern that at present is as low in the public opinion as it can well get, and there is a good deal to be said, both for and against. I would like to put it on its feet but it means giving up a great deal to do so. I believe I would get the loyal support of all interested in the concern, and this is a great deal, but it would mean a great deal of hard and worrying work, to say nothing of having to do many unpleasant things; still, it is a great opportunity.

Ned Bewind called this afternoon, and said he hoped I would accept Morgan's proposition. I told him it was so entirely different to what I contemplated that it would need careful consideration. He said he hoped I would give it favourable consideration.

It is a most difficult situation, and I hope you will assist me in coming to a decision, as all I want to do is for the best for all concerned. My feeling is to tell Morgan I propose returning home on the 24th instant, and that with the understanding I shall not be expected to spend more than three to four months here, say from middle January to middle of May, and that if he is prepared to give me

£20,000 a year to begin with, that I will favourably consider his proposition; but before coming to a decision I
wish to talk the matter over with you, and that within a
week of my arrival home will cable him definitely, and that
if my answer is in the affirmative, I will return to America
within two weeks, and undertake the responsibility of re-
organising the I.M.M. Co. This will give me ample time to
think over the matter, hear my mother's and your views,
and do not think this delay will in any way be to the detri-
ment of the I.M.M.

I feel the matter is of so serious a nature that it is not one
in which a hurried decision can be expected, and I am anxious in both our interests to have the opportunity of talking
over the matter with you, and possibly Pirrie.

I may say that Morgan is much down on Pirrie and stated
that if the combine had not gone through he would have
been bankrupt six months ago, as he could not have carried
the load he had on his shoulders.

I think I have written you fully, and explained the position
and do not know I can add anything more.

Yours very sincerely,

[Signed] J. Bruce Ismay

It can be seen from this letter, namely the cable referred to,
that Bruce Ismay took the opinion of his mother Margaret
very seriously, just as his late father Thomas had done. Harold
Sanderson visited Margaret as requested, and she wrote her
encouraging reply to her son the same day:

Dawpool,
Thurstaston,
Birkenhead

My Dearest Bruce,

Mr. Sanderson telephoned this morning saying he had received an important cable from you, and that he thought he had better come out and see me. Mr. Imrie and Amy were coming out to lunch, so I asked Mr. Sanderson to come with them, which he did, and after lunch, he read your cable to me. It was much as I expected except in one thing, which of course is a great blow to me that you must be in America half your time, but while deeply regretting this, I must put personal feelings on one side for I know it is a proud and important position you are offered, and you naturally wish to see the great undertaking in a prosperous condition, and for this to be so, I feel that you are the only one whose management can achieve this.

I think your own inclination is to accept, and I do not wonder at it, for it is well known what exceptional power you have. I am sure you will have given the subject deep and anxious consideration, and we can only trust that whatever decision you arrive at, that it will be the right one. I have every confidence that it will be, in the natural course of events, you have a large part of your life before you, and I hope you may be spared to bring the great concern with which you are so deeply interested to a successful issue. We must not forget that you are asked to give up many important interests on this side, for I suppose you will not be able to retain the North Western, or your other directorships. I am sorry at this, for I had it in my mind that railway work was what you would take up as your interest later on, for I should like to think that you will have some leisure in your lifetime.

Mr. Sanderson cabled you early this evening, so I expect before you receive this your decision is made.

I don't think there is anything more to say; I shall look anxiously for further news, trusting that you and Florence are well. With much love, ever dearest Bruce,

Your loving Mother.

February 10th, 1904.

After receiving a telegram from Sanderson, conveying his and Margaret's initial thoughts on the matter, Bruce wrote the following letter to Sanderson:

9, Broadway,

New York.

February 11th, 1904.

My dear Harold,

I yesterday received the following cable from you, viz.:-

'Have been Dawpool consult Mrs. Ismay. We both are disappointed that should be required divide your time between England and States, but feel you should not regard this condition as insuperable, if otherwise your inclination is to accept. Hope can be arranged residence in States reduced to minimum and seasonable periods.'

And am glad to see therefrom that you have been to Dawpool to talk over the matter with my mother. It is most difficult to arrive at a conclusion as to what is the best course to pursue and I am hopeful of being able to arrange to postpone giving any answer until I have had an opportunity of discussing the matter with you. Steele is, I know, anxious for a reply, as he telephoned me yesterday, asking if I had anything to say to him.

The idea of spending much of my time in America is not congenial to me, but if I could arrange to limit it to say, three months, it would not be so bad.

I hoped your cable could have given me some indication as to what are your views, but you do not do so, merely telling me I should not consider the proviso of living in New York insuperable if my inclination is to accept. I think you know that if I had considered my own inclination and feelings absolutely, I should, in all probability, have resigned ere this, but I am trying to look at the matter from a general point of view, and whether by taking the position, even for a limited period, would be to the benefit of all concerned. If I should accept, it means my having to give up a good deal personally, and sever my connection with the L. & N.W. Railway, and all outside companies in which I am interested. The railway I always considered would give me occupation for my old age. If I give it up now, I could not expect to get on the board at some future time, say five years hence.

However, there is really nothing I can add to what I have already written you, and nothing has developed since. I saw Morgan on Tuesday; in fact, I did not see any of them yesterday.

I am going to Boston tomorrow with Lee, and hope to get back on Saturday evening.

Assuming I can get Steele to agree to my not coming to any decision until I have had a talk with you at home, I shall in all probability get away by the Celtic; failing this I will return by the Cedric, as I have quite given up all idea of visiting the Mediterranean this time.

Trusting all is working smoothly, and that you are all well.

Yours very sincerely,

J. Bruce Ismay.

Harold A. Sanderson, Esq.,
30, James Street,
Liverpool.

From this letter, it would seem that even at this early point in negotiations over presidency of IMM, Bruce considered that his time as the head of the combine may be relatively short. The purpose of his visit to Boston was twofold: first, he wished to visit *Republic*, which was in port at that time, second, he wanted to experience the port at first hand.

On 15 February 1904, Bruce sent a very long letter to Sanderson. The letter has several headings, two of which are included below. Heading 3, 'Cunard Line', mentions *Carpathia*, the Cunard liner which would, in years to come, rescue survivors of the *Titanic* disaster, including Bruce Ismay. Heading 11, 'Boston', describes Ismay's visit to Boston and *Republic*. Bruce was not overly impressed by his experience:

My dear Harold,

3. Cunard Line

The memorandum of the conversation you had with Moorhouse is interesting. I think they will hesitate before bringing about a demoralization of rates.

I am curious to see what effect Ballin's action will have on the Cunard people. He intends taking strong measures, and I am quite in accord with him. It is a good thing the freight is being put up by a German Line, and is not a so-called British one; it will ease the situation for us.

The Cunard are evidently going to do their utmost to improve their position, and I cannot help feeling they have got hold of a live man somewhere; as you know I have often mentioned this. It is showing itself in many directions.

I hear they intend altering the Ultonia and she will run with the two new steamers in the Mediterranean, the Aurania and Carpathia being the extra boats in the New York trade, leaving them with the Saxonia and Ivernia only in the Boston trade, excepting the Sylvania (no passengers).

11. Boston

I went over to Boston with Lee on Friday morning, reaching there at 3 p.m., and at once went to the Republic.

The wharf is not an ideal one from which to work a first-class passenger business, but there is room for much improvement in their present practise.

The new officers are, I think, good, and there should be no difficulty in the organisation thereof, but at present they are all sixes and sevens. I cannot say I was favourably impressed by Mr. Britton, and time will show if he is the right man.

We dined on board the Republic, and I was much surprised to find that Captain McAuley had three friends to dinner and the doctor too; surely they know this is strictly against our rules!

I saw the ship away at 8 a.m. on Saturday; she was somewhat late owing to some of the firemen being absent.

She was in a dreadful state of dirt, largely owing to the use of the ash ejector, which had smothered her with ashes, and owing to the severe weather it was not possible to clean her.

On leaving the wharf she had no one in the look-out bridge, no fog horn was sounded to warn visitors of her departure, no United States mail flag was flying from the mizzen, and a canvas save-all was hanging over her side. The screens on the promenade deck were half up and half down. They should have all been down and stowed away.

Her departure was most unsatisfactory, and most discreditable to all concerned. There was no one from the office to see her away; in fact, the whole thing was as bad as it could well be.

Please write Captain McAuley for an explanation on the several points mentioned. If he cannot maintain the discipline we must have, he is not the man we want.

Steele called at the hotel yesterday afternoon, and I had three hours with him, going over the same ground. We are, generally speaking, in accord as to what should be done. He is anxious I should come to some decision with reference to the presidency, but, appreciating the seriousness of the step does not wish to unduly press me. He repeated how very anxious Mr. Morgan and himself were I should accept his offer.

This morning I sent you the following cable:-

'Steele unwilling unduly press for reply, but anxious for decision. Assuming I do not consider American residence insuperable, is it mother's and your opinion I should accept. Very difficult decide; Steele, Morgan and others most anxious should accept. I hesitate taking such important step. Would much like you cable definite advice after receiving letter Oceanic.'

I hope to receive some definite advice on receipt of my letter per Oceanic and am writing Steele to the effect that I will give him a decided answer on Thursday.

It is most difficult to know what is the best thing to do, there is so much to be said on both sides; but if I only considered myself, I would decline the responsibility. Of course, should I accept, it means you would have a great deal more on your shoulders, as I could not possibly give the same close attention to White Star business in the future as in the past, and we must always bear in mind that the White Star is the most important part of the business, and must be kept up to its present efficiency.

I fully expect to get away from here on the Cedric, and will cable you as soon as I can what my movements will be. Of course, if I accept the Presidency, it will be necessary for me to return almost immediately, so as to begin organising the staff here on the lines that I have suggested, and which meet the approval of Steele, Franklin and Lee.

Trusting you are all well, and that matters are working smoothly at the office,

Yours very sincerely,

Bruce Ismay

Harold A Sanderson Esq.,
30 James Street,
Liverpool.

The Leyland Line had become part of International Mercantile Marine in 1902, but it was soon considered that the manager, Mr Wilding, was not operating in the best interests of the IMM combine. Many directors of the combine felt that the Leyland Line was continuing business as if it were an independent company, much to the annoyance of the heads of IMM, and to Bruce, which he mentions in a letter which he sent to Harold Sanderson:

9, Broadway,
New York,
February 19th, 1904.

My dear Harold,

Your cable of the 17th inst., duly reached me, reading as follows:-

'Been Dawpool. We feel that provided financial position offers no bar, you would do well to accept; but would suggest, as matter is of great importance you should endeavour if practicable carry out your idea of giving decision after arrival home and discussion here.'

and after thinking the matter over, I sent you on the same day this message, viz.:-

'My letter Oceanic fully explained position, nothing new transpired since. Under these circumstances, hardly think a further discussion Liverpool would throw fresh light on situation, or assist in reaching decision. Having regarded your views, propose accepting before sailing Wednesday. Cable if you agree.'

And on the 18th the following cable came to hand:-

'Quite agree, only mentioned delaying actual acceptance thinking that your own wish.'

I do not really think that any good purpose would be served by deferring coming to a decision until my return home, and hardly think further discussion would throw any fresh light on the subject.

I have sent a note to Steele advising him that when he has expressed his willingness to agree to the terms and conditions of which I am prepared to fall in with his wishes, and can give me some absolute and definite assurance that the Leyland Line is under the control of the I.M.M. Company, I will give him my answer:-

The position assumed by the Leyland Line is extraordinary, and it is necessary to know if they were controlled by the I.M.M. Company or not, and a cable has been sent by Steele to Dawkins, telling him to see Wilding and clear up this position. Their action fully bears out a statement made by Roper to you and myself viz.:- that the Leyland Line was quite prepared to work in harmony with the I.M.M. Company so long as it suited him to do so, but if the interests of the I.M.M. Company were contrary to the interests of the Leyland Line, then it was his business to protect the interests of the Leyland Line, even if in so doing he was injuring the

I.M.M. Company. Their action with reference to the freight agreement, and now their refusal to withdraw tonnage from the Boston-Liverpool berth, is quite in accord with, and fully bears out Roper's contention, and Bray has been the means of rendering the I.M.M. Company ridiculous in the eyes of the steamship world generally.

I told Steele yesterday that unless the situation was cleared up, and the position of the Leyland Line towards the I.M.M. clearly defined, neither I nor anyone else would, I should think, be prepared to accept the position of president of the I.M.M. Company.

I am now waiting to hear from Steele; in the meantime my sailing is getting very close, and nothing done, so far. It is the same old plan of leaving things until the last moment, and then trying to rush them through.
Griscom still away, but I understand he is progressing, and now out of bed.

I think the Continental lines should have consulted the British lines before putting out an $18 prepaid Scandinavian rate, and so cabled you. While we agree to their putting on this line as a tentative measure, I certainly had in mind that they would concur with us before taking any step.

The Italian business is in a state of absolute demoralisation and the outlook of passenger business generally most gloomy. We have decided this morning to quote an East bound Italian rate of $22.00, less $2 commission. I suggested to Boas it would be well to reduce at once to $10 and he agreed, and so cabled Ballin, who replied he feared if we did this, the Italian Government might claim that if we could carry Italians one way for $10 we could do so both ways. I am of opinion the only way to bring matters to a head is to make things as bad as possible, and then people will be more willing to come to some agreement.

We hope to receive a cable from you today advising us as to the decision arrived at by the Cunard directors.

I had a talk with Vernon on Wednesday. He was very friendly, but we did not discuss matters in any detail. He strongly urged me to take up the I.M.M. Co., and says he believes it can be made a financial and commercial success.

Trusting all goes on smoothly, and that you are all well.

Yours sincerely,

J. Bruce Ismay.

Harold Sanderson, Esq.,
30, James Street,
Liverpool.

After much consideration and advice from his family, friends and business acquaintances, many of the latter he also considered as close friends, J. Bruce Ismay decided to accept the offer of presidency of IMM and sent the following letter to Charles Steele accordingly:

Holland House,
New York,
February 21st, 1904.

Dear Steele,

Referring to the interview we had at Mr. Morgan's house on Tuesday, the 10th inst., when Mr. Morgan, Mr. Griscom and yourself were present, at which I was offered and requested to accept the presidency of the International Mercantile Marine Company; having given the matter my earnest and most careful consideration, have decided to fall in with the wishes of Mr. Morgan and yourself, and am prepared (subject to the understanding contained in the memorandum agreed with you yesterday, and subsequently approved by Mr. Morgan, being executed, and the letter written with reference to the Leyland Line), to assume the duties and responsibilities of the position.

There is no doubt the I.M.M. Company is at present in an extremely unsatisfactory condition, both in regard to finance and organisation, and you will appreciate it will require a great deal of hard and anxious work to put it on a proper working basis; but this I am prepared to undertake, feeling, as I do, that I have the goodwill and confidence of Mr. Morgan and yourself, and that I can count on you both to assist me in every way that lies in your power to attain the end we all have in view.

I would like to say, had I consulted my own feelings in this matter I should, without the slightest hesitation, have declined the offer; and have been very largely influenced in my decision by a desire to render any assistance I can to Mr. Morgan and yourself to place the I.M.M. Co. in a satisfactory position, and although it may be a long and hard road to travel, I believe if we all work heartily and loyally together, that ultimately we shall meet with some measure of success.

Thanking you for all your kindness and courtesy, and hoping we have many years of pleasant co-operation before us.

Yours sincerely,

J. Bruce Ismay.

Chas. Steele, Esq.,
34, West 49th Street,
New York City.

The following is a copy of the memorandum that Bruce had drawn up and mentioned in his letter to Mr Steele:

MEMORANDUM of the understanding under which J. Bruce Ismay is willing to consider undertaking the duties of President and Managing Director of the INTERNATIONAL MERCANTILE MARINE COMPANY.

It is understood:-

1. That J. Bruce Ismay shall have the title of president and managing director.
2. That his management of the business of the I.M.M. Company shall be unlimited and uncontrolled, and his decision on all points other than financial matters must be final:
3. That the entire control of all the subsidiary Companies of the I.M.M. Company shall be vested in him, and that his decision on all matters of policy and management of these Companies shall be final so far as the I.M.M. Company can control the same.
4. That he shall have the absolute power of appointing and dismissing, without any appeal, any persons in the employ of the I.M.M. Company, or any of the subsidiary companies so far as the I.M.M. Company can control the same.
5. That all the companies in which the I.M.M. Company has an interest shall be subject to and conform to his instructions, and that such instructions shall be final so far as the I.M.M. Company can control the same.
6. That he will receive the hearty and loyal support and co-operation of those most largely interested in the welfare of the I.M.M. Company.
7. That he shall arrange to have a residence in New York, the time it may be necessary he should reside in America being left absolutely to his judgment and discretion.

8. That the business in America and Canada, and the West Indies shall be conducted in such manner as he may think best.

9. That he shall be at liberty to resign the position at any time; by giving six months' notice, and conversely the board shall have the right to call for his resignation on like notice.

10. That he shall receive as a remuneration for filling this position the sum of $50,000 per annum, in addition to the compensation now received by him from the White Star Line, and as a member of the British committee and voting trustee.

11. That Mr. Morgan is prepared, in the event of the earnings of the I.M.M. Company and subsidiary companies not being sufficient to meet the fixed charges of the I.M.M. Company and subsidiary companies, to advance the monies necessary to make good any deficiencies for a term of three years after January 1st, 1904.

12. That Mr. Morgan undertakes the above liability on the understanding that the net earnings of the I.M.M. Company and subsidiary companies will be allocated first to pay such charges.

13. Mr. Morgan is willing, in the event of the earnings of the I.M.M. Company and subsidiary companies being in excess of the amount necessary to meet the fixed charges of the I.M.M. Company and subsidiary companies, that any surplus is to be allocated to meet the indebtedness of the I.M.M. Company and subsidiary companies to Harland and Wolff, before being obliged to any indebtedness that may be owing to his firm.

14. That the finance committee shall in no way control or interfere with the prerogatives of the president and managing director, as set forth in this memorandum.

15. Finally, it is distinctly understood that the board of
    directors, the finance committee, and those who may
    control the destiny of the I.M.M. Company and the
    subsidiary companies are prepared to give unlimited
    control in all matters to, J. Bruce Ismay, and are willing
    to place absolute and entire confidence in him in
    every respect, subject only to the powers of the finance
    committee regarding financial matters, and the power
    of the board to call for Mr. Ismay's resignation as
    hereinbefore stated.

[Signed] J. Pierpont Morgan.
P. A. B, Widener.
Charles Steele.

After accepting the office of president of the International
Mercantile Marine Company, Bruce, along with his wife
Florence returned home to Liverpool aboard *Cedric*. They
departed New York on 24 February 1904, during which time
Bruce received a cable from Sir Clinton Dawkins (head of the
IMM British Committee). Bruce replied to Sir Dawkins once
Cedric had reached Queenstown, known today as Cobh:

On board R.M.S. Cedric,
March 2nd, 1904.
(Off Queenstown).

Dear Sir Clinton,
    It was extremely pleasing to receive your very welcome
message, reading as follows:-
    'Our most sincere congratulations. We all look forward to
many years pleasant work with you, and assure you of our
hearty and full co-operation.'

It is unnecessary to say how much I appreciate the kind thought that prompted you to so cable.

I was in a very difficult position in New York, and the decision arrived at was largely influenced by the strong personal pressure, brought to bear on me by Mr. Morgan, Mr. Steele and several others of our American friends. Had it not been for this and had I purely consulted my own feelings, nothing would have induced me to accept the position of president of the I.M.M. Company, as I had looked forward in the near future to a life of ease and enjoyment.

However, having accepted the very onerous and responsible post, it is my intention to do all in my power to place the I.M.M. Company in a different position to the extremely unenviable one in which it now stands, and it is most satisfactory to feel I can rely on having the hearty and full co-operation of Pirrie, Wilding and your good self.

It would be idle on my part to hope to accomplish anything unless I felt I had the sympathy of all interested in the I.M.M. Company, and my recent visit to America assured me such was the case there, and you will readily understand how gratifying it was to receive similar assurance from you here.

I cannot say I am at all sanguine as to the future of the I.M.M. Company, but if we all work loyally together for its welfare, we may, in years to come, attain some measure of success, but we have a long and difficult road to travel.

At the present time there seems to be a state of war in every trade in which we are engaged, and, in both the passenger and freight branches of the business the outlook being most discouraging. However, we must put our backs into it and try to rectify matters as soon and as much as possible.

It is my present intention to return to the States as soon as possible, as I am anxious to see the carrying out of the organisation already decided upon, but hope, before doing so, to have an opportunity of discussing matters with you.

Steele talked of coming over for a week, sailing from New York on the 9th inst, and returning in time to allow Mr. Morgan to leave on April 6th, and my movements will, to a certain extent, be influenced by what he decides to do.

Messrs. Morgan and Steele were extremely kind to me during my stay in America, and I much appreciate the full and absolute control they have placed in my hands, and it will be my endeavour to prove to them that their confidence is not misplaced.

Mr. Morgan seems determined, so far as lies in his power to do everything possible to put the I.M.M. Company on its feet, and make it a commercial success, and we, on our part, must lend him every assistance to attain this end.

Trusting you are all very well, and with renewed thanks for your kind message, believe me,

Yours sincerely,

J. Bruce Ismay

Sir Clinton R. Dawkins, K.C.B.,
22, Old Broad Street,
London, E.C.

It may be assumed from this, and from the previous letters, that Bruce was somewhat reluctant to accept the position as president of IMM, and he was already thinking about his retirement from the shipping world. However, as he had made an agreement with the IMM, he would, for the time being, do all in his power to make the combine a world leader in the movement of both passenger and freight.

Once Bruce arrived in England, he was met with a myriad of communications congratulating him on taking up presidency

of IMM. Letters and cables were received from family, friends
and business acquaintances alike, including letters from his sisters Ethel and Charlotte:

'Farnborough Hall,
Banbury.

My dearest Bruce,

Just a few lines to welcome you home, and to congratulate you very much on the splendid position that you have
accepted, you must feel very proud. I am afraid it means
harder work than ever, and I heard it does not mean residing
permanently in New York as the papers said. Don't trouble
to answer this. Mother and Lottie will tell me your plans.
I hope you left Florence well and that you will find the
children quite well. We came here on Saturday and return
home today.

Very much love dearest Bruce, and all good wishes for success in the difficult work that lies before you.

Your loving sister,
Ethel
Feb. 29, 1904

Moor Park,
Ludlow.
March 1st, 1904

My dearest Bruce,

I must send you a line to congratulate you upon being
made President of the I.M.M. Co.

I am afraid it means a great deal of hard work, and our
great drawback as far as we are concerned is that you will be
away from England so much, and we shall miss you dreadfully.

It will be very nice to see you and I do hope you are coming to Dawpool over Sunday.

I came here yesterday for the races but there is too hard a frost and they have abandoned. I wonder what sort of voyage you have had!

Looking forward to seeing you soon,

Lottie

While in negotiations over the presidency of IMM, the undesirable state of the company, especially its financial position had become very apparent to Ismay. On accepting the presidency, Bruce believed that he could, given sufficient time, greatly improve the financial situation and believed that the White Star Line would become a major part in achieving this goal. He also felt that if IMM was to be successful, it was imperative that all managers and partners should work closely together, so on 2 March 1904, just one week into his presidency, Bruce wrote the following letter to Lord Pirrie, who was instrumental in placing Bruce in the highest managerial position at IMM:

March 2nd, 1904
(off Queenstown)

My dear Pirrie,

Your kind message reading as follows:-

'Our most sincere congratulations. We all look forward to many years pleasant work with you, and assure you of our hearty and full co-operation.'

reached me on board of the Cedric the day I left New York, and it is hardly necessary for me to say how very much I appreciate the kind thought that prompted you to send same, and how gratified I was to receive the assurance of your hearty and full co-operation.

You will readily understand I did not accept the position of President of the I.M.M. Co. without giving the matter earnest and careful consideration, and had I purely considered my own feeling, would without hesitation, have declined same, but finding Mr Morgan, Mr Steele, Mr Griscom and many other friends interested in the I.M.M. Co. with very strong views as to what I should do, eventually acceded to their request. I may say that in coming to this decision I was largely influenced by personal feelings and also by the fact that I felt I should receive the hearty, loyal and active cooperation of all connected with the I.M.M. Co., for without this it would be quite impossible to hope to achieve any measure of success.

We must all realise that the fortunes of the I.M.M. Co. are at an extremely low ebb, and it means a great deal of anxious and hard work to pull it through, and although I am not at all sanguine as to the future of the company, believe if we all work together, and do all possible in the interests of and for the welfare of the I.M.M. Co., that in years to come we may possibly see some slight return for our efforts, but the immediate future is surrounded with serious difficulties.

The most pressing one, to my mind, is the question of finance, and it is in this respect that you can give us much assistance and relief. I know the Company is largely indebted to your Firm, and we must do all possible to reduce this liability; all I ask is that you should make it as easy as possible, and not press us unduly. I do not think there is the least ground for any uneasiness on your part, as no doubt in time the indebtedness will be wiped out, and no one is more alive to the present position than Messrs Morgan and Steele, who are quite prepared to allow your claims on the I.M.M. Co. to be considered as prior indebtedness to that of the Company to their Firm.

It was most pleasing to me to see the evident determination on the part of Mr Morgan to make the I.M.M. Co. a success, if possible, and he is, I am sure, willing and anxious to do all in his power to attain this end.

It is my present intention to return to America at the earliest moment possible, (in fact, I may manage to get away on the Cedric next Wednesday, but must, of course be guided somewhat by what I find calling for my attention at James Street), as I am anxious to get matters on a sound basis in America, and have already arranged for a good many radical changes being carried out. It will be necessary; I expect that I should remain in the States for four or five weeks.

I should not, of course, like to leave England again without seeing you, as there are many matters I wish to discuss with you, and hope we may arrange a meeting.

In the meantime, things are generally as bad as they can be, and the outlook gloomy in the extreme. We are in a state of war in the Mediterranean trade, in the Atlantic trade both passengers and freight, (the Provision rate being 3/- per ton), and much fear from my latest advices that we are in for a serious upheaval in Australia and New Zealand, but shall do everything possible to avert the latter.

Steel's movements are somewhat uncertain. He talked of leaving New York per Oceanic on 9th inst., to spend a week in England, returning in time to allow Mr. Morgan to sail on the 6th April, and I must be guided somewhat as to my movements by what he decides.

Well, I have undertaken a big job, and look to you to help me all you can, and feel sure I can rely on your loyal and hearty help and support. Again thanking you for your kind cable, and trusting Mrs. Pirrie and you are well, and with my kindest remembrances to both.

Believe me,

Yours very sincerely,
J. Bruce Ismay

The Right Hon. W.J. Pirrie, LLD., D.Sc.,
Queen's Island,
Belfast.

The cause for Ismay's concern lay in the 1904 IMM financial report, which demonstrated net earnings of $4,000,522, with net expenses of $3,645,227. IMM's surplus earnings balance for that year being just $355,295. Bruce Ismay felt that this was a small amount for such a large business, even after allowing for the 1903 depression in North Atlantic freight; he felt that this figure could be greatly improved. Almost immediately, Bruce made many changes throughout the IMM combine, including increased responsibility for the managers and efficiency at all levels, especially on the American side. His enthusiasm, charisma and loyalty infused solidarity among his managers.

One year into Bruce's presidency, the 1905 financial report was already indicating that the IMM was growing in strength; the surplus was showing almost ten times that of the previous year. This change of management and subsequent favourable financial report no doubt reassured investors. While it is almost certain that the end of the North Atlantic freight depression played its part in the increase of profit, there is little doubt that Ismay taking presidency of the combine also had a very positive effect. The following extract of a letter from Pirrie to Ismay, written one year earlier, on 27 February 1904, demonstrates Pirrie's confidence in Bruce Ismay:

My heartiest congratulations on your appointment to the position of President of the I.M.M. Co., an appointment that I have long felt was essential to the success of the combination, and from the first and second interview I had with Mr. Morgan I have been looking forward to seeing you occupy it. A single controlling genius was what we wanted and now that we have this I am sure everything will go satisfactorily. Personally I feel gratified that the memorandum we drew up is being accepted so pleasantly by the Americans.

You must have been very busy and I am sure much worried to know what was best to do considering the difficulty in connection with the Leyland Line and other little matters cropping up. As regards the Leyland matter I think all will come out right in the end. Until we meet I need not bother you with details, but I believe that in Wilding and Dawkins you will have very loyal colleagues thoroughly determined to do the best they can in this and every other difficult position. Under your regime, however, I anticipate that we will be able to avoid most of the difficulties that arose in the past.

At the beginning of 1907, the decision was made that many of the fastest vessels of the White Star Line fleet, which were employed on the North Atlantic trade, could run from Southampton rather than Liverpool, largely owing to the fact that the new port was closer to London and the European ports. In May of that year, *Celtic* departed from Southampton on a trial voyage, with it being deemed a huge success. Consequently, one month later, *Adriatic* was the first White Star vessel to take this new commercial service. *Oceanic*, *Teutonic* and *Majestic* would join *Adriatic* to make up a quartet, while *Celtic* would continue to operate to and from Liverpool.

One evening, during the summer of 1907, Bruce, along with his beloved wife Florence, went to dine with Lord and Lady Pirrie at their home, Downshire House, Belgrave Square, in London. It is often said that during this dinner the two gentlemen conceived the idea of building two new ships in response to Cunard's *Lusitania*, which was now nearing completion, but initial plans for these two gigantic new ships had been discussed long before 1907. This can be evidenced by the enormous new Thompson graving dock at the Belfast shipyard. Construction of the dock began in late 1904, the same year that Bruce became president of IMM. This new dock was constructed to accommodate White Star's largest ships, which would become known as the Olympic class, they were to be given the names *Olympic* and *Titanic*, with the option of a third ship to follow.

It is conceivable that during their dinner, Ismay and Pirrie agreed on further details and specifics that would be added to their existing plans. The new Olympic class would never rival the new Cunard ships in terms of speed but were designed to exceed all other ships in size, comfort and safety, combined with operational economy.

These great leviathans of the sea could have been given to any shipping line of the IMM combine, but Bruce insisted that they should sail under the flag of the White Star Line for several reasons. Ismay wanted White Star to remain the most prestigious line of the IMM combine. He saw the existing White Star ships as his family's ships and wanted them to receive the best care. It was well known at the time that *Oceanic* (1899), the last ship to be completed during his late father's lifetime, received a generous share of Bruce's personal attention with regards to maintenance, repairs and improvements. Additionally, White Star Line's long relationship with the shipbuilders Harland & Wolff meant that the line was better established than any other shipping line within the IMM combine.

The vision for the future was that *Majestic* and *Teutonic*, both now ageing ships, would be taken into reserve and the 'Big Four', as they were known, *Adriatic*, *Baltic*, *Cedric* and *Celtic* would be used on the Liverpool service. *Oceanic* would join

Olympic and *Titanic* on the Southampton service until the last of the three sister ships, *Britannic*, was put into service and would substitute for whichever of her two sisters was in dock for overhaul.

Facing colossal build costs, the White Star Line issued an additional £1.5 million worth of shares, which were quickly bought up. Investment was also needed at Harland & Wolff's shipyard in Belfast. Three existing slipways needed to be removed and replaced by two much larger slipways, which would be covered by a complex gantry known as the Arrol Gantry.

Work commenced on *Olympic*, and soon afterwards, *Titanic*. The two sister ships were built side by side; they must have been a marvellous sight, towering high above the nearby houses.

In the meantime, Harland & Wolff had been busy building two more ships for the White Star Line: *Megantic* and *Laurentic*, both intended for the Canadian trade. *Megantic* was given two quadruple expansion engines, making her a twin-screw steamer, while *Laurentic* was given a new type of propulsion system, this being a pair of reciprocating engines driving two wing propellers, while exhausting into a low-pressure turbine which drove the centre propeller, making *Laurentic* a triple-screw vessel. *Laurentic's* new engines had proved superior to that of *Megantic*. *Laurentic* was more powerful, capable of a slightly higher speed and was economical in comparison. This new propulsion system would be adopted for the Olympic class of vessels and became the new Harland & Wolff standard for many years to come.

Since the very beginning, the White Star Line had always believed in the importance of training ship's officers, especially for working under sail, and it was around this time that Bruce decided to introduce a new training ship. In 1908 he purchased an iron-hulled ship built in 1894 by Charles Connell of Glasgow. *Mersey* was a 1,829-ton sailing ship, 270ft in length with a beam of 39ft, thus making her ideal for the purpose that Bruce had intended.

Mersey had the distinction of being the first sailing vessel to be equipped with a wireless. She was also the first sailing ship aboard which an operation for appendicitis was performed. Under the command of Captain Corner, *Mersey* voyaged all over the world until she was sold by Harold Sanderson at the outbreak of the First World War.

It was also around the same time that Bruce Ismay decided that White Star employees should have access to a super-annuation fund. This was unusual in 1908, but he felt that many of the staff, both on land and at sea, would be glad of a pension in their later years. He, therefore, started the fund, initially for the office staff, which was operated through the Royal Insurance Company, the idea being that once the scheme was well established and proved satisfactory, it would be extended to the officers of the White Star Line. It was always the intention to do this, but in view of the sinking of *Titanic* in 1912 and the retirement of J. Bruce Ismay just over one year later, the scheme for the officers never materialised.

7

RMS *OLYMPIC*, FIRST
OF THE OLYMPIC CLASS

O lympic was the pioneer of White Star Line's new Olympic class of ships, closely followed by *Titanic* and, soon afterwards, *Britannic*. The keel of *Olympic* was laid down on 16 December 1908 and was given Harland & Wolff's Yard Number 400, with the keel of *Titanic* being laid three months later, being designated Yard Number 401.

Olympic and *Titanic* had originally been designed with three funnels, but both White Star and Harland & Wolff agreed that an additional funnel should be added to the specifications. The additional funnel would help ventilate the engine-room, galley and First Class smoking areas; it would also symbolise power and stability.

Both ships were built side by side, amid the intricate steel-work of the purpose-built Arrol Gantry, which was named after its builder, Sir William Arrol. These two new ships were of similar size, with *Titanic* being a little over 1,000 tonnes heavier on completion.

Work on both ships proceeded with all haste, with the construction of *Olympic* taking almost two and a half years to complete. Although all three sister ships were designed to carry North Atlantic passenger trade between Southampton and New York, *Olympic* was the only one that would complete the Atlantic crossing.

Olympic was launched on 20 October 1910. It was never standard practice for White Star Line vessels to be christened at launch, and this revolutionary new ship was no exception. At launch, *Olympic* was not much more than an empty shell with the propelling mechanisms already installed. The hull and superstructure were painted light grey for photographic purposes, this being common practice of the White Star Line for the first of a new class of ships.

Once the launching ceremony was over, the new vessel was moved to the Thompson graving dock, which had been specially built to accommodate the new liners as fitting-out work was completed. A host of highly skilled craftsmen, including boilermakers, electricians, plumbers and carpenters, were deployed to make the ship ready for sail day, this mammoth task being completed in only seven months.

Two days of sea trials were carried out, beginning on 29 May 1911, after which the Board of Trade issued a certificate of seaworthiness. The first of the three leviathans of the sea was now ready for White Star Line service.

The day *Olympic* was handed over to the White Star Line was a great day for White Star and for Harland & Wolff. It was no coincidence that, on the same day, the second of the sister ships, *Titanic*, was launched. Bruce Ismay attended the launch, along with his eldest daughter, Margaret, with many prominent people also in attendance, including J. Pierpont Morgan.

After seeing *Titanic* safely launched, the whole company of invited guests sailed from Queens Island to Liverpool on board *Olympic* and were immediately impressed by her size, stability and power. On arrival in Liverpool, Bruce and his daughter disembarked and returned to Sandheys, and *Olympic* was then open for public inspection, the proceeds being given to local hospitals.

The press were busy reporting the news of the two great sister ships, which together represented over 90,000 tonnes of shipping. Credit was given to the White Star Line for their great undertaking and also to Harland & Wolff for the building of these two ships. The cost of building *Olympic* and *Titanic* was around £3 million, equivalent to around £356 million today. *Olympic* was some 14,000 tonnes larger than the world's previous largest liner, the Cunard Line's *Mauretania*.

After the brief stay at Liverpool, *Olympic* sailed to Southampton to make ready for her maiden voyage to New York. The ship was still receiving a huge amount of publicity – much more than her younger sister *Titanic* would receive at the start of her maiden voyage the following April. Bruce Ismay travelled to Southampton to join *Olympic* for the maiden voyage, accompanied by his wife, Florence.

Olympic commenced her maiden voyage on 14 June 1911, under the command of Edward John Smith, who would lose his life almost one year later during the *Titanic* disaster. From the observations he made during the voyage, Bruce noted several recommendations that were then incorporated into the sister ship, *Titanic*. Notably, the forward section of 'A' deck promenade was open to the elements, and the same section on *Titanic's* 'A' deck was subsequently enclosed by windows, to name but one.

On arrival at New York, Bruce Ismay sent a cablegram to Lord Pirrie:

Olympic is a marvel, and has given unbounded satisfaction.

Once again accept my warmest and most sincere congratulations.

Will cable you full particulars speed, consumption later.

He later sent a letter to his head office, an extract of which is given below:

9, Broadway,
New York.
June 22nd, 1911.

Messrs. Ismay, Imrie & Co.,
30, James Street,
Liverpool.

Dear Sirs,

I was very pleased indeed to be able to send to you the following cable message on Wednesday last:-

'Arrived at Lightship 2.24, docked at 10 a.m. everything worked most satisfactorily, passengers delighted. Passage 5 days, 16 hours, 42 minutes, average speed 21.7; coal consumption given 3,540, think it liberal estimate. Delayed by fog 1½ hours. Daily runs 428, 534, 542, 525, 548. Single ended boilers not lighted.

Communicate this to Pirrie, Harland, Belfast.'
which I now have to confirm.

Everything on board the ship worked most satisfactorily, and the passengers were loud in their praises of the accommodation and table.

The machinery worked excellently, and there was no hitch of any kind in connection with same.

The consumption has been extremely low, averaging, as far as I can make out, about 620 tons a day instead of

720 as anticipated and we arrived here, with approximately 1,300 tons of coal on board the ship. I am arranging to have the ship fully coaled for the return trip, including the reserve bunker, so as to reduce the quantity required to be taken at Southampton.

At no time during the passage were the engines working at full speed, the highest number of revolutions being 79 port and 81 starboard, at which speed the ship was practically quiet. On the passage home we expect to work her up to full speed. The five single ended boilers were not used at all during the passage out.

The most popular room on board the ship was, undoubtedly, the Reception Room, as it is always crowded after lunch, at tea time and after dinner and we cabled you requesting you to communicate with Messrs. Harland & Wolff, asking them to order 50 additional cane chairs and ten tables for this room.

The after companion-way between the Lounge and Smoking room on 'A' deck was practically not used at all, and I think we must again consider putting state rooms in this space; but I propose to watch this matter carefully on the voyage home to see what use is made of the accommodation for the large number of passengers on board.

The deck space, with the number of passengers on board going out, was certainly excessive, and I think, in another, ship we might carry out the rooms on 'B' deck the same as those on 'C' deck.

I also cabled, asking you to arrange for a potato-peeler in the crew's galley, as it was felt desirable one should be placed there, and also one of Phillips water tube steam ovens for the bakehouse, of the largest capacity possible to increase the output, as experience shows that the oven at present in the ship is not capable of producing sufficient bread daily.

Finding that there were no holders for cigars or cigarettes in the W.C.s we cabled you, asking you to arrange to supply these, so that they can be fitted before the next voyage.

The only trouble of any consequence on board the ship arose from the springs of the beds being too springy, this, in conjunction with die spring mattresses, accentuated the pulsation in the ship to such an extent as to seriously interfere with passengers sleeping, and we cabled, asking you to communicate with Pirrie that if he sees no objection, we would like to have lath bottoms fitted before the next voyage, and hope this can be arranged.

The trouble in connection with flic beds was entirely due to their being too comfortable.

Finding that the service from the pantry to the saloon could be satisfactorily carried out through one door on each side, we have arranged to close the other doors, which will enable us to put in two additional tables in the Saloon, giving an increased seating capacity of eight people.

It came to my knowledge that some people had been down in the engine Room during the passage from Southampton to Cherbourg. I therefore wrote to Mr. Bell in regard thereto, and herewith enclose you his reply. I am sure you will share my surprise that Mr. Willett Bruce and Mr. Blake should feel themselves justified in giving permission to the gentleman named to visit the Engine Room and I shall be glad if you will ask them for their explanation for so doing.

Mr Bell wrote his reply to Bruce the same day:

Mr. Ismay
R.M.S. Olympic at Sea.
June 14th, 1911.

Sir,

In reply to your inquiry regarding visitors to Engine Rooms, I beg to state that three gentlemen have been in Engine Room during the passage from Southampton all by Mr. Blake's instruction, viz. Mr. Van Eldon and two gentlemen connected with a French Steamship Company, whose names I do not remember, but whom Mr. Blake said had been sent to him by Mr. Willett Bruce,

Another gentleman presented himself this morning saying that Mr. Currie had instructed him to come to me, but I refused him permission on his verbal statement.

Your instructions shall be strictly obeyed.

I am, Sir,

Your obedient servant,

J. Bell, Chief Engineer.

Chief Engineer Bell was the same Joseph Bell who would later serve and give his life on *Titanic's* maiden voyage.

It can be seen from this letter that Bruce Ismay paid very close attention not only to the mechanical workings of the ship, but also to the comfort and satisfaction of passengers. It is also apparent that on her first Atlantic crossing, the White Star Line's newest flagship *Olympic* was never required to run at full speed during her maiden voyage, although this was a consideration for the return trip from New York to Southampton.

Olympic soon settled into her regular transatlantic crossings, which, for three months, passed largely without incident of any kind. This changed on 20 September 1911, as *Olympic* was beginning her fifth regular voyage from Southampton.

While making her way down the Solent, under the command of Captain E.J. Smith, and the direction of Trinity House pilot, Mr G. Bowyer, *Olympic* encountered the British cruiser HMS *Hawke*, which was close by and running in a near-parallel position. In order to navigate Bramble Bank, Bowyer reduced speed from 17 to 11 knots. The wide turn took HMS *Hawke's* commander, William Blunt by complete surprise, and subsequently, he was unable to take sufficient action to avoid colliding with *Olympic*. HMS *Hawke's* bow had been designed to sink enemy ships by ramming them and had collided with *Olympic's* starboard side. It was by good fortune that nobody was killed in the incident. Although *Olympic* sustained major damage, she managed to steam back to port on just one engine, a damaged propeller shaft and two watertight compartments open to the sea. *Hawke* suffered severe damage to her bow and almost capsized.

A long legal battle ensued, which concluded that *Olympic* was at fault, even though the ship was technically under the control of the Trinity House pilot. This result meant that the White Star Line faced huge legal costs, along with a very expensive repair bill, together with loss of revenue while *Olympic* was out of commission. The incident was heavily reported by the press. As *Hawke* had been designed to sink enemy ships by ramming them with her bow, the very fact that *Olympic* had survived the collision seemed to fuel the claims that *Olympic* was virtually unsinkable.

After temporary repairs lasting two weeks had been carried out at Southampton, *Olympic* sailed to Belfast for permanent repairs in the Thompson graving dock, where several new hull plates were fitted. In order to expedite repairs, *Titanic's* starboard propeller shaft was used to replace that which had been damaged on *Olympic*. As construction of *Titanic* had to be partially halted, and her starboard propeller given to her older sister, the maiden voyage of *Titanic* was delayed by three weeks, with her original date being altered from 20 March 1912 to 10 April that year.

★★★

One year after the *Hawke* incident, *Olympic* was once again returned to her Belfast builders. Her owners decided that major safety improvements should be carried out, mainly because of the lessons learned following the *Titanic* disaster. Additional davits were installed to allow the ship to carry an additional forty-eight lifeboats, raising her number of lifeboats from twenty to sixty-eight. Five watertight bulkheads were extended up to 'B' deck, with a subdivision included in the electrical dynamo room (the purpose of this room was to generate and distribute electricity throughout the ship). In addition to this, a double hull was created by the installation of a watertight floor in the engine and boiler rooms. Finally, improvements were made to the ship's pumping equipment.

It was calculated that *Olympic* would now stay afloat with six of her watertight compartments open to the sea. This was a huge refit, yet *Olympic* was ready to re-join the White Star fleet and sail for New York on 2 April 1913. By the time she returned to service, *Olympic* had retained the enviable title of the world's largest ship, but this title would soon be taken by the German-built *Imperator*, launched in June of the same year.

Over a year later, with Bruce Ismay now retired from the White Star Line, *Olympic* was about to join other White Star vessels, including *Celtic, Cedric, Oceanic* and *Teutonic*, as they were integrated into the Admiralty at the outset of the Great War.

When war broke out, *Olympic* was on a regular voyage from Southampton to New York. On arrival, the ship's standard White Star Line colours were covered with several coats of grey paint. Portholes were also covered in the hope that the ship would be less visible to the new enemy. *Olympic* returned with only her crew on board.

Normally, *Olympic* would have returned to the regular port of Southampton, but this was quickly changed to Liverpool, her port of registration. Before arrival, the destination was changed again, this time to Glasgow, responding to rumours that German U-boats were on patrol in the English Channel and the Irish Sea.

Olympic continued with her regular crossings for a short while, mainly to accommodate Americans who were trapped in Europe and eager to return home. By contrast, eastbound voyages carried very few passengers.

Declining passenger traffic eventually led to a decision to withdraw the ship from passenger service. At the end of October 1914, *Olympic* left New York bound for Glasgow, on what would be her final commercial voyage during the war years. She had her full complement of crew and a mere 153 passengers. While passing Ireland's north-west coast, *Olympic* received distress signals from Her Majesty's battleship *Audacious*, which had struck a sea mine and was heavily taking on water. *Olympic* was requested to stand by and be ready to assist with the evacuation of the crew of *Audacious*, eventually rescuing her 600 crew. *Olympic* was diverted to Belfast, where passengers experienced a lengthy wait before being allowed ashore in an attempt to delay the news of the loss of *Audacious*.

With the war now gaining momentum and civilian transatlantic passenger trade declining sharply, the White Star Line decided it was no longer viable to retain *Olympic* in service and so she was laid up in Belfast for almost a year before being chartered by the British Admiralty for use as a troopship for the duration of the war. In order to fulfil her new purpose, great changes were needed to make room for the transportation of up to 6,000 troops, as opposed to her usual 2,600 passengers.

As a precaution and for the safety of those on board, *Olympic* was armed with one 12lb gun forward and a 4.7in gun aft. For the duration of her wartime service, *Olympic* became officially known as HMT (Hired Military Transport) *Olympic* with the transport number T2810.

HMT *Olympic* made countless voyages to New York, Canada and the Mediterranean, during which time the ship and crew were involved with many rescues and campaigns, including the withdrawal from Gallipoli. On 12 May 1918, *Olympic* gained the distinction of being the first recorded merchant transport ship to sink a German U-boat.

After the Armistice agreement in November 1918, *Olympic* was charted by the Canadian Government to carry troops back to their home country, returning to Belfast in August of the following year for a major refit, so that she could resume her normal peacetime Atlantic service. The post-war refit included a modernisation of the interior fittings and the conversion of her boilers to allow the burning of oil instead of coal. This conversion meant that *Olympic* could operate with only sixty engine-room personnel, which compared favourably to the previous complement of 360 staff. This conversion also allowed the refuelling time to reduce from days to hours.

After the war *Olympic* provided many years of faithful service, but with the Great Depression of the 1930s, followed by the emergence of larger and faster liners such as the German-built SS *Bremen* and Italy's SS *Rex*, the popularity of *Olympic* began to fall. In 1934 the White Star Line was merged with the Cunard Line and the title Cunard White Star Line was adopted for a brief while before reverting back to the previous title of Cunard Line, six years later. One year after the merger, *Olympic* was retired and laid up at Southampton until she was purchased six months later by Sir John Jarvis.

Upon completion of the sale, *Olympic* was towed to Jarrow where, for a period of two years, her superstructure was demolished, after which the hull was towed to Inverkeithing for final demolition.

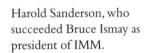
TS *Mersey.*

Harold Sanderson, who
succeeded Bruce Ismay as
president of IMM.

Olympic passing the Isle of Wight. (Courtesy of the Beken Archive)

Titanic beginning her maiden voyage. (Courtesy of the J. Kent Layton Collection)

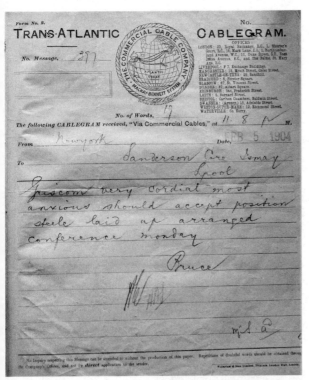

Cablegram from Bruce Ismay to Harold Sanderson while he was considering the presidency of IMM.

Form No. 2. No.

TRANS-ATLANTIC CABLEGRAM.

No. Message, 297

No. of Words, 17

The following CABLEGRAM received, "Via Commercial Cables," at 11 8 — M.

From _New york_ Date, FEB 5 1904

To _Sanderson Care Ismay Lpool_

Griscom very cordial most anxious should accept position steele laid up arranged conference monday

Bruce

The first of two cablegrams from Bruce Ismay to Harold Sanderson after being offered the presidency of IMM.

Form No. 2. No.

TRANS-ATLANTIC CABLEGRAM.

No. Message, 24

No. of Words, 103/98

The following CABLEGRAM received, "Via Commercial Cables," at 12 37 A M.

From _New yrk_ Date FEB 10 1904

To _Sanderson Carl Ismay Lpl_

Had meeting morgan steele griscom present offered me presidency and unlimited control morgan thinks my residing here portion each year absolutely

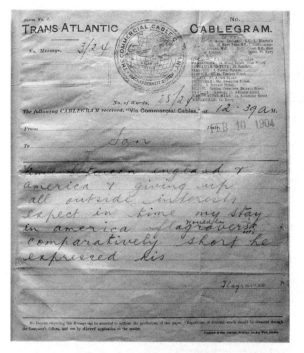

The second of two cablegrams from Bruce Ismay to Harold Sanderson after being offered the presidency of IMM.

Richard Fry, Bruce Ismay's valet, was lost during the *Titanic* disaster.

COPY OF AGREEMENT

DATED   February 23rd   1904

A G R E E M E N T

RE

PRESIDENCY OF

INTERNATIONAL MERCANTILE MARINE COMPANY

MEMORANDUM of the understanding under which J. Bruce Ismay is willing to consider undertaking the duties of President and Managing Director of the International Mercantile Marine Company.

It is understood

1. That J. Bruce Ismay shall have the title of President and Managing Director.

2. That his management of the business of the I. M. M. Co. shall be unlimited and uncontrolled, and his decision on all points other than financial matters must be final.

3. That the entire control of all the subsidiary Companies of the I. M. M. Co. shall be vested in him, and that his decision on all matters of policy and management of these Companies shall be final, so far as the I. M. M. Co. can control the same.

4. That he shall have the absolute power of appointing and dismissing, without any appeal, any persons in the employ of the I. M. M. Co., or any of the subsidiary Companies, so far as the I. M. M. Co. can control the same.

5. That all the Companies in which the I. M. M. Co. has an interest shall be subject to and conform to his instructions, and that such instructions shall be final so far as the I. M. M. Co. can control the same.

6. That he will receive the hearty and loyal support and co-operation of those most largely interested in the welfare of the I. M. M. Co.

7. That he shall arrange to have a residence in New York, the time it may be necessary he should reside in America being left absolutely to his judgment and discretion.

8. That the business in America and Canada, and the West Indies, shall be conducted in such manner as he may think best.

-2-

9. That he shall be at liberty to resign the position at any time, by giving six months' notice, and conversely the Board shall have the right to call for his resignation on like notice.

10. That he shall receive as remuneration for filling this position the sum of £30,000 per annum, in addition to the compensation now received by him from the White Star Line and as Member of the British Committee and Voting Trustee.

11. That Mr. Morgan is prepared, in the event of the earnings of the I. M. M. Co. and subsidiary Companies not being sufficient to meet the fixed charges of the I. M. M. Co., and subsidiary Companies, to advance the moneys necessary to make good any deficiency for a term of three years after January 1, 1904.

12. That Mr. Morgan undertakes the above liability on the understanding that the net earnings of the I. M. M. Co. and subsidiary Companies will be allocated first to pay such fixed charges.

13. Mr. Morgan further is willing, in the event of the earnings of the I. M. M. Co. and subsidiary Companies being in excess of the amount necessary to meet the fixed charges of the I. M. M. Co. and subsidiary Companies, that any surplus is to be allocated to meet the indebtedness of the I. M. M. Co. and subsidiary Companies to H. & W. before being applied to any indebtedness that may be owing to his firm.

14. That the Finance Committee shall in no way control or interfere with the prerogatives of the President and Managing Director, as set forth in this memorandum.

15. Finally, it is distinctly understood that the Board of Directors, the Finance Committee, and those who may

-3-

control the destiny of the I. M. M. Co., and the subsidiary Companies are prepared to give unlimited control in all matters to J. Bruce Ismay, and are willing to place absolute and entire confidence in him in every respect, subject only to the powers of the Finance Committee regarding financial matters, and the power of the Board to call for Mr. Ismay's resignation, as hereinbefore stated.

(Signed) J. PIERPONT MORGAN }
F. A. B. WIDENER } Voting Trustees
CHARLES STEELE }

J. P. MORGAN & CO.

Copy of Bruce Ismay's agreement for accepting the presidency of IMM.

Bruce and Florence Ismay aboard *Teutonic*, 1889.

DAWPOOL.
THURSTASTON,
BIRKENHEAD.

My dearest Bruce

Mr Sanderson telephoned this morning saying he had received an important cable from you & that he thought he better come out & see me, Mr Imrie & Amy were coming out to lunch. so I asked Mr Sanderson to come with them. which he did & after lunch. he read

your cable to me. it was much as I expected except in one thing. which of course is a great blow to me. that you must be in America half your time. but while deeply regretting this. I must put personal feeling on one side. for I know it is a proud & important position you are offered. & you naturally wish to see the great undertaking in a [prosperous?] condition. & for this &

I feel that you are the only one whose management can achieve this. I think your own inclination is to accept. & I do not wonder at it for it is well known what exceptional power you have. I am sure you will have given the subject deep and anxious consideration & we can only trust that whatever decision you arrive at. that it will be the right one. I have every confidence that it will be. in the natural course of events you have a large part of your life before

Letter sent to Bruce from his mother, expressing her personal thoughts over the presidency of IMM.

you. & I hope that you
may be spared to bring
the great concern with
which you are so deeply
interested to a successful issue.
We must not forget that
you are asked to give up
many important interests
on this side. for I suppose
you will not be able to
retain the North Western
or your other directorships —
I am sorry at this, for I had
it in my mind that railway
work was what you would
take up as your interest later
on — for I should like to
think that you will have
some leisure in your life time —

Mr. Sanderson called
you early this evening.
so I expect before you
receive this your decision
is made — I don't think
there is anything more
to say — I shall look
anxiously for further news
trusting that you and
Florence are well. & with
much love —
Ever dearest Bruce
Your loving Mother
Oct 10th.

Margaret's letter continued.

BOAT DECK

Detailed drawing of *Titanic*'s Boat Deck. (Courtesy of Bruce Beveridge)

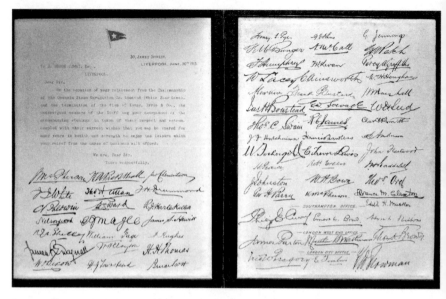

Letter of appreciation signed by members of staff, following Bruce's retirement from the Oceanic Steam Navigation Company.

Bruce Ismay with his gardener, Hughie, in the grounds of Costelloe Lodge, Ireland, around 1932.

Costelloe Lodge, Ireland, after the 1925 rebuild.

Mr and Mrs Bruce Ismay at Costelloe, looking west across the North Atlantic.

The wreck of the *Titanic.*(Courtesy of RMS Titanic Inc., Georgia, USA)

8

RMS *TITANIC*

While *Olympic* was in Southampton, soon to depart for another voyage to New York, *Titanic* was about to leave Queen's Island, Belfast, ready to commence her sea trials. The White Star Line's newest and largest ship departed on the 2 April at 6.00 a.m. after being delayed for a day due to poor weather conditions. It must have been an amazing sight, seeing her four funnels and upper decks towering high above the Belfast skyline as the ship made way through Belfast Lough and into the Irish Sea.

After aligning her compasses, the world's largest ship steamed south, toward the Isle of Man, under the command of Captain Herbert Haddock. *Titanic* performed marvellously, much to the delight of those on board. During her sea trials, several speed tests and manoeuvres were carried out which also demonstrated that the ship could come to a dead stop within the required distance.

Representatives on board included Harold Sanderson, on behalf of the White Star Line, and Edward Wilding, along with Lord Pirrie's nephew, Thomas Andrews, a brilliant young naval architect who had been heavily involved with the construction of *Titanic*. Wilding and Andrews were representing the ship-builders Harland & Wolff.

During the trials Andrews was busy monitoring every aspect of the ship. He had replaced *Titanic*'s chief designer Alexander Montgomery Carlisle, who had recently retired. The chairman of Harland & Wolff, Lord Pirrie, had wished to be present during the sea trials, but as he was in poor health, his doctor had prohibited him from attending.

Also on board were two Marconi operators, Jack Phillips and Harold Bride, who were kept busy, fine-tuning the Marconi equipment. Below decks was a skeleton crew of seventy-eight greasers, stokers and firemen, known as the Black Gang. A further forty-one crew members included officers, senior crewmen, cooks and storekeepers.

At the end of her satisfactory sea trials, *Titanic* returned to Belfast, arriving at 6 p.m., with one final test being required – the lowering of the ship's port and starboard anchors, which was successfully carried out. After obtaining her seaworthiness certificate, anyone not travelling to Southampton was ferried ashore, including Wilding and Mr Carruthers, surveyor for the Board of Trade.

Two hours later, *Titanic* left Belfast for the last time and steamed toward Southampton. Time was of the essence as it was essential that the ship should arrive at Southampton for the midnight high tide on Wednesday, 3 April.

Titanic was advertised to depart Southampton on Wednesday, 10 April, but in 1912 the United Kingdom was experiencing its first national coal strike. The ship had sailed from Belfast with a little over 6,000 tonnes of coal, which was considered to be just enough to complete her voyage in ideal weather conditions, but insufficient if the ship experienced bad weather or other delays.

While making way from Belfast to Southampton, a small fire was detected in No. 10 coal bunker, situated on the starboard side of boiler room No. 6. This was not uncommon in those days and was not considered to be a threat to the safety of the ship or those on board, but the fire was not helpful to the limited coal supply. The odds were already against the ship, so it was considered prudent that the coal supply should be increased. This was achieved by taking coal out of White Star Line's *Oceanic* and the American liner *New York*, the outcome being that both these ships were laid up.

While in Southampton, Mr Thomas Andrews wrote a letter to his wife expressing his delight with the ship, saying that he had a great deal of work to do before the ship sailed. Meanwhile, Bruce Ismay and his wife Florence drove from their London home, accompanied by three of their children, Tom, Evelyn and George, with Florence at the wheel of their large Daimler Landaulette. This was one of the very few long car journeys Bruce undertook, as he disliked motoring so much, especially at speed.

As with many *Titanic* passengers, they stayed the night at Southampton's South Western Hotel. Bruce was in great spirits, having only two weeks earlier seen his eldest daughter Margaret joined in matrimony to Mr George Ronald Cheape, and now he was about to board the White Star Line's latest and largest ship, *Titanic*. While previously on board the sister ship *Olympic*, Bruce had noted several points for improvement, which were subsequently incorporated into *Titanic*'s design – he was now looking forward to seeing how popular they would prove to be.

It being the Easter holidays, it was decided that Bruce would sail alone. Florence felt that as her husband was sailing to New York, then returning soon afterward, she would spend time with their children, as their stay at home would be short before returning to school. Bruce, Florence and their three children boarded *Titanic* on 10 April at 9.30 a.m. to see at first hand the opulence of this beautiful new ship, especially Bruce's accommodation, suite 52–56 on 'B' deck. This parlour suite was originally to be occupied by J.P. Morgan, financier of IMM, but as he was unable to travel, it was then allocated to Ismay.

Once Mrs Ismay and the children had looked around, they returned to the dockside to see the magnificent ship, along with her husband, depart for New York. Afterwards, Florence and the children left Southampton to take a motoring tour of Devonshire and Wales.

Under the command of Edward J. Smith, *Titanic* had arrived in Southampton with a skeleton crew of just over 100, which was considered ample for her journey from Belfast to Southampton. During her stay in the White Star Dock (later renamed Ocean Dock), the remaining crew were signed on.

The day before *Titanic* left port, Henry Tingle Wilde was signed on as chief officer, making him Captain Smith's second in command. Wilde had been chief officer on *Olympic*, working alongside Captain Smith. Both Smith and Wilde had been part of the Royal Naval Reserve, and some thought it was no surprise when Officer Wilde was chosen to accompany Captain Smith during what would be his very brief command of the White Star Line's latest vessel.

The appointment of Henry Wilde caused a reshuffle of the previously appointed officers. William McMaster Murdoch had previously been appointed as chief officer, and consequently, he was demoted to First Officer, which also resulted in Charles Herbert Lightoller being demoted from First Officer to Second Officer.

As a result of these changes, the previous Second Officer David Blair, who had been with *Titanic* during her sea trials, was quickly transferred to the White Star liner *Adriatic II* for a brief period until he joined the officers of *Oceanic II*. In the rush, Blair had taken the keys to the locker where the binoculars were stored, which had been intended for use by the lookouts. There has been much controversy over the results of this action, with many claiming that the binoculars would have enabled the lookouts to see the iceberg much sooner, and therefore disaster might have been avoided. Recent scientific studies have suggested that due to the unusual temperatures on the evening of 14 April 1912, the use of binoculars would probably not have made any significant difference to the sequence of events of that night.

At twelve noon, RMS *Titanic* left Southampton, beginning her maiden voyage to New York, but her departure was not without incident. The magnificent ship was initially towed by five tugboats, before the mighty propellers turned, and *Titanic* moved forward under her own steam. Due to the coal strike, many ships were laid up in Southampton Docks, slightly obstructing the deep channel that *Titanic* was meant to follow.

As the mighty ship was increasing speed, the suction from the propellers was becoming greater. At that moment, *Titanic* passed the *New York*, the force being so great that *New York*'s moorings broke, causing the ship to drift out into *Titanic*'s path. Only the quick thinking of the master of the tug *Vulcan* prevented a collision. The prompt action of those on board *Titanic* also helped as the order 'full astern' was given, and the starboard anchor was lowered as a precaution. A collision was avoided by only a couple of feet, and many saw this near miss as a bad omen.

Titanic entered and crossed the English Channel without further incident, arriving at Cherbourg, France, about six and a half hours later, where she took on board more passengers and mail, which were delivered by the tender ships SS *Nomadic* and SS *Traffic*. At around 8 p.m., the mighty vessel left Cherbourg and headed for Queenstown, Ireland, arriving at 11.30 the following morning, again taking on more passengers and mail.

This was to be *Titanic's* final scheduled stop before crossing the North Atlantic.

Two hours after arriving at Queenstown, the world's largest vessel departed for New York. *Titanic* began her Atlantic crossing carrying a grand total of 2,208 passengers and crew, which was a considerable number short of her total carrying capacity.

While at Queenstown, Chief Engineer Joseph Bell had been invited to Bruce Ismay's cabin to discuss the expected coal consumption for the entire voyage. Bruce's wish was for the coal to be conserved and that the ship was not to be forced. However, they did agree that if Captain Smith approved, and if the weather was favourable, a speed trial should be conducted during the afternoon of the following Monday or Tuesday.

During the subsequent United States Senate Inquiry, Senator Smith questioned Bruce about the speed of *Titanic* during the North Atlantic crossing. As part of his answer, Ismay stated, 'It was our intention, if we had fine weather on Monday afternoon or Tuesday, to drive the ship at full speed. That, owing to the unfortunate catastrophe, never eventuated.'

This was possibly one source of the rumours that suggested Ismay had interfered with the navigation of the vessel and that *Titanic* was travelling at full speed, although the latter has since been disproved. Another source of this rumour is possibly due to a conversation that Elizabeth Lines claims she overheard. At the American Limitation of Liability hearings, Mrs Lines stated that on the Saturday afternoon, 13 April, she overheard a conversation between Smith and Ismay. Elizabeth Lines told Mr Frederick Brown, representing the counsel for claimants, that she overheard Ismay saying to Captain Smith, 'We will beat the *Olympic* and get in to New York on Tuesday'.

Soon afterwards, Mrs Lines was questioned by Henry Duke, counsel for the petitioner. When asked to describe the appearance of Smith and Ismay, she was unable to describe either of the men. Although Mrs Lines stated that she had never seen Captain Smith prior to witnessing this conversation, she also stated that she had previously seen Bruce Ismay while he was living in New York, thirteen years earlier. Mrs Lines further testified that she was uncertain of the identity of the man speaking with Smith, saying, 'I am afraid I could not describe Mr Ismay'. This statement probably explains why Mrs Lines had earlier asked a steward to confirm Ismay's identity. Mrs Lines' inability to accurately describe Smith and Ismay may have been due to the fact that she gave her testimony eighteen months after the *Titanic* disaster.

Meanwhile, *Titanic* steamed across the North Atlantic using the Southern Track – this was the appropriate course for ships crossing the North Atlantic between the months of January to July. The Northern Track is some 200 miles shorter, thus making a faster crossing, but during these months, the large amounts of ice would usually present a grave danger to shipping. By contrast, the Southern Track is generally considered to be much safer because the ice floes travelling down the Labrador Current would normally break up in the Gulf Stream. This particular year saw an exceptional amount of ice travelling along the Labrador Current. The Arctic winter had been especially mild, resulting in much larger amounts of ice, with the ice travelling much further south than usual, consequently presenting a far greater danger to ships, including those using the Southern Track.

Passengers on board the White Star Line's latest vessel were settling in, with those of all three classes enjoying life on the magnificent ship, as she flawlessly steamed toward New York at an average speed of 21 knots. Some had booked passage on *Titanic* in order to experience this wonderful new ship and to enjoy the famous White Star Service, a standard of service that was regarded as being above all others. For many more passengers, *Titanic* presented an opportunity to begin a wonderful new life in America.

Among the many emigrants hoping for a new and better life were fourteen men and women from Addergoole, a small village situated on the shores of Lough Conn, County Mayo, Ireland. As with many other emigrants, their hearts were full of hopes and dreams of a promising new life in America.

One of the 'Addergoole 14', as they are now better known, was Patrick Canavan. Pat was 22 years old when he boarded *Titanic* at Queenstown and was destined for Philadelphia, Pennsylvania. It had been arranged that he would initially live with his sister, Kate, who is likely to have been among the crowd waiting for *Carpathia*'s arrival after the rescue of the *Titanic* survivors. Like so many others, Kate would soon learn that her brother was among the missing. One survivor of this group was Annie Kelley. She later described how she witnessed Pat Canavan and John Bourke directing their small group of Third Class passengers towards an iron ladder, leading them to the upper decks. Young Pat's body, if recovered, was never identified.

On the morning of 14 April, *Titanic* received the first of six ice warnings, with the Cunard liner *Caronia* reporting 'bergs, growlers and field ice'. This message was acknowledged by Captain Smith. Shortly after 1.30 p.m., a second message was received by the ship's radio operators, this time from White Star Line's *Baltic*. They had relayed an ice report from SS *Athinai* advising that she was passing icebergs and large quantities of ice. This message was also acknowledged by Captain Smith, who also showed the message to Bruce Ismay.

Just a few minutes after the report from *Baltic*, a message was transmitted from Hamburg-America Line's SS *Amerika*, which was situated a short distance to the south of *Titanic*'s position. This message never reached Captain Smith or any of the senior officers. The fourth ice warning was received at 7.30 p.m. from Leyland Line's *Californian*. The short message simply read 'three large bergs' and gave their position as 42.3° N 49.9° W.

Californian's message was followed two hours later by a message from *Mesaba*, belonging to the Atlantic Transport Line. This message read, 'In latitude 42° N. to 41° 25' N., long. 49° to 50° 30' W. Saw much heavy pack ice and a great number large icebergs. Also field ice. Weather good; clear'.

By this time, *Titanic*'s second radio operator, Harold Bride, had retired for the night, leaving Jack Phillips alone at the Morse key. Phillips may have overlooked the significance of the message from *Mesaba* because he was busy transmitting messages for passengers via the relay station at Cape Race, Newfoundland. The radio set had broken down the previous day and had taken several hours to repair, resulting in a backlog of messages which the radio operators were trying to clear. Perhaps it was for this reason that the message also failed to reach the bridge.

Throughout the day there had been talk of ice in *Titanic*'s vicinity, but passengers placed their complete trust in Captain Smith, along with his crewmen. The plummeting temperature had long since driven most passengers away from the promenade decks, preferring the warmth of the various saloons and of their cabins. Many of the Third Class passengers had been dancing and singing in the General Room, where a piano was provided for their entertainment, before later retiring to their own cabins. Meanwhile, in Second Class, Reverend Ernest Carter had organised a hymn service with more than 100 passengers attending. The two-hour service ended at 10.00 p.m. with the majority of passengers leaving for their cabins soon afterwards. In First Class, small groups of passengers had formed their own select parties within the dining room before dispersing into the lounges and the smoke room, with the majority eventually retiring to their cabins and suites.

The sixth and final ice warning was received at 10.30 p.m., sent by Cyril Evans, the 20-year-old radio operator of *Californian*, which had come to a standstill in an ice field some miles away. This message read, 'We are stopped and surrounded by ice.' Phillips interrupted and signalled back, 'Shut up, keep out, I'm working Cape Race'. Again, the vital message never reached the bridge. *Californian* carried only one wireless operator, and he went off duty soon after sending his message to *Titanic*.

In 1912, ice warnings were generally treated as advisories rather than calls to action. It was generally believed that ice presented little danger, and it was not unusual for the commander of a vessel to continue at a good rate of speed. It was widely known that a ship would best respond to the helm when travelling at speed, as this would ensure a good flow of water over the ship's rudder, this being standard practice at that time.

The weather conditions that *Titanic* encountered during the evening of 14 April were exceptional. The sea was an almost perfect calm and the night was extremely clear, the stars were bright, yet no moon was visible. This unusual combination made it extremely difficult to see far ahead, even with the ever-watchful eyes of the lookouts.

As the huge ship was approaching her final hours, most passengers had settled into their beds, and the air temperature had quickly fallen to near freezing. Having satisfied himself that all was well, Captain Smith gave orders that a sharp lookout should be kept. He also stated that if visibility worsened, the ship should be slowed and he should be called immediately. He then retired to his cabin, leaving First Officer Murdoch in charge of the bridge.

Frederick Fleet and Reginald Lee were the two lookouts on duty that evening, diligently keeping watch for anything in *Titanic's* path, especially ice. The lookouts' binoculars were not available due to the earlier mix up in Southampton, when Officer Blair was transferred to another ship, taking the key to the binocular locker with him.

At 11.39 on the evening of 14th April, Fleet spotted a large iceberg directly ahead of *Titanic*. As soon as he saw it, he rang the lookout's bell three times and then reached out for the telephone, which was connected to the ship's bridge. He frantically turned the telephone handle, which generated a small electrical current, enough to ring the telephone bell on the bridge.

Alerted by the bell, Sixth Officer James Moody picked up the receiver without saying a word. Fleet finally had to ask, 'Are you there?'

Moody replied, 'Yes, what do you see?'

Fleet anxiously replied, 'Iceberg right ahead!'

We will probably never know if this short delay affected how long Murdoch waited before ordering the evasive manoeuvre. Moody thanked Fleet for his report before relaying the message to First Officer Murdoch, who then ordered the helmsman, Quartermaster Robert Hichens, to turn 'hard a-starboard'. Soon afterwards, Murdoch set the ship's telegraph to stop. The colossal ship began to slowly turn, but *Titanic* was too close to the iceberg, and a collision was inevitable.

Although a head-on collision had been avoided, the forward part of *Titanic's* starboard side had collided with the huge mass of ice beneath the waterline. The iceberg was later estimated to weigh 1.5 million metric tonnes.

Murdoch rang the electric warning bell to alert those in the lower compartments that the watertight doors were about to close and the switch to initiate closure was activated after a short delay. Fourth Officer Boxhall arrived on the bridge moments after the collision, finding that Captain Smith was already there.

Smith had been alerted by the ringing of the bell by the lookouts, and he had also felt the impact of the ship scraping past the berg. Smith anxiously asked First Officer Murdoch, 'What have we struck?'

Murdoch quickly confirmed that they had struck an iceberg and followed with his report on the action already taken. Smith and Boxhall walked to the starboard bridge wing to look aft of the ship but could not clearly see the iceberg. Smith instructed Boxhall to conduct a visual inspection of the forward part of the ship below decks, then report back to him. While waiting for Boxhall's report, Smith moved the ship's telegraphs to 'Half Ahead' then soon afterwards to 'Stop'.

On completion of his inspection, Boxhall returned to the bridge and reported to the captain that he could see no damage. Smith instructed him to find the ship's carpenter and get him to sound the ship. Boxhall met the carpenter on a staircase as he was heading towards the upper decks. The carpenter hastily informed him that the ship was taking on water, before proceeding to the bridge to make his report to the captain. Meanwhile, Boxhall decided to assess the damaged cargo area. Finding the mail room flooded, he quickly realised that the situation was far worse than he had initially thought.

At this time, the remaining deck officers were becoming uneasy as they waited to hear news of any damage to the ship, while those below in Forward Boiler Room 6 had little doubt as to the seriousness of the situation, as water began flooding in between the hull plates, about 2ft above the floor level.

Now realising that the ship was very seriously damaged, Fourth Officer Boxhall hurriedly returned to the bridge and made Captain Smith aware of the dire situation. Smith carried out his own inspection, in order to personally assess the damage, after which he gave the order for the covers to be taken off the lifeboats, at this point hoping that it would be only a precautionary measure. He then instructed Boxhall to go to the chart room and calculate the ship's position, which was recorded as 41° 46' N 50° 14' W, a position later proved to be inaccurate by around 12 miles. After making his captain aware of the ship's position, Boxhall was sent to the Radio Room, where he communicated *Titanic's* position to the radio operator.

At the time of the collision, Bruce Ismay was sleeping in his cabin, B52–56, and was alerted by a sudden vibration. Thinking that the ship had lost a propeller blade, Bruce left his cabin and went into the passageway where, meeting a steward, he asked what had happened. The steward told him that he did not know. On hearing this, Bruce walked back to his cabin, put on an overcoat and made his way to the bridge where he found Captain Smith. Upon realising the *Titanic* had struck ice, Bruce asked Smith if the damage was serious. Smith replied, 'I'm afraid so.' After hearing the troubling news, Bruce made his way to the Boat Deck, where passengers were beginning to gather, as preparations to load the lifeboats were underway. Initially, Bruce found himself beside lifeboat No. 7, located on the starboard side. Under the supervision of First Officer Murdoch, this was the first lifeboat to be lowered from the stricken vessel.

Several crew members later testified that they witnessed Bruce Ismay assisting with preparing and loading lifeboat No. 7, including Bedroom Steward Henry Samuel Etches. At the American inquiry, he stated under oath:

> Mr. Ismay, in the first place, was asking the gentlemen to kindly keep back, as it was ladies first in this boat; and they wanted to get the boat clear first. The gentlemen were lined up, those that were trying to assist, and Mr. Ismay said, 'Kindly make a line here and allow the ladies to pass through.'

Mr William Ward, saloon steward, also testified that he witnessed Mr Ismay assisting with this lifeboat.

Once lifeboat No. 7 had begun to be lowered, Bruce Ismay made his way to starboard lifeboat No. 5. On arrival, he found First Officer William Murdoch was again in charge, and he attempted to assist in any way he could, just as he had done with the previous lifeboat. Mr Henry Samuel Etches was again present. When questioned by Senator Smith, he stated:

> Mr. Ismay called out twice, I know, in a loud voice – 'Are there any more women before this boat goes?' and there was no answer. Mr. Murdoch called out; and at that moment a female came up whom I did not recognise. Mr. Ismay said: 'Come along; jump in.' She said: 'I am only a Stewardess.' He said: 'Never mind, you are a woman, take your place.' That was the last woman I saw get into No. 5 boat, sir.

Mr Alfred Crawford, also questioned by Senator Smith, stated:

> I went on the starboard side to No. 5 boat. I saw Mr. Murdoch and Mr. Ismay helping to get the passengers in. They were calling out and assisting all the women into the boat. Mr. Ismay stopped Mr. Murdoch from lowering the boat a bit because the after end was getting hung up. Mr. Murdoch called out to the aft man that was lowering the fall to lower away all the time, that he would beat him, and they lowered the boat to the water.

Fifth Officer Harold Lowe was also working at lowering lifeboat No. 5. At the American inquiry, Lowe made the following statement regarding some strong language which he shouted out to Bruce, not realising who he was:

The occasion for using the language I did was because Mr. Ismay was over anxious and he was getting a trifle excited. He said, 'Lower away! Lower away! Lower away! Lower away!'

I told him, 'If you will get to hell out of that I shall be able to do something.'

I said, 'Do you want me to lower away quickly?'

I said, 'You will have me drown the whole lot of them.'

Officer Lowe's stern words reminded Bruce Ismay that while on board *Titanic* his position was the same as any other passenger. Having no real authority, he made no reply, turning and walking away. During the same inquiry, Third Officer Pitman told Senator Smith:

Then this man in the dressing gown said we had better get her loaded with women and children. So I said, 'I await the commander's orders,' to which he replied, 'Very well,' or something like that. It then dawned on me that it might be Mr Ismay, judging by the description I had had given me. So I went along to the bridge and saw Captain Smith, and I told him that I thought it was Mr Ismay that wished me to get the boat away, with women and children in it. So he said, 'Go ahead; carry on.' I came along and brought in my boat. I stood on it and said, 'come along ladies'. There was a big crowd. Mr Ismay helped to get them along; assisted in every way. We got the boat nearly full, and I shouted out for any more ladies.

Almost one month later, at the British inquiry into the *Titanic* disaster, Officer Lowe presented a slightly shorter statement than that which he had originally made at the American inquiry.

When asked by Mr Cotter if Bruce was giving any orders, he replied, 'No, he was trying all in his power to help the work, and he was getting a little bit excited. I told the men to go ahead clearing No. 3 boat, and Mr. Ismay went there and helped them.'

Third Officer Pitman had met Bruce at lifeboat No. 5 and was also questioned at the British inquiry. Mr Butler Aspinall asked, 'Did you see Mr Ismay close to this boat?'

Pitman replied, 'I did.'

Aspinall then asked if Mr Ismay said anything.

Pitman replied, 'He remarked to me as we were uncovering the boat, "There is no time to lose." Mr Ismay remarked to me to get it filled with women and children.'

After seeing lifeboat No. 5 safely away, Bruce moved to No. 3 lifeboat, where he was joined soon afterwards by Officer Harold Lowe. Officer Lowe testified at the American inquiry that on his arrival at lifeboat No. 3, he saw Bruce Ismay already there, assisting.

First Class Bathroom Steward Samuel Rule was also assisting with lifeboat No. 3. When questioned by the attorney general at the British inquiry, Rule stated, 'Mr Ismay was seeing them [passengers] into No. 3 boat; he was just the same as any of the crew; he was doing all he could to assist to get the boats out.'

The next lifeboat to be prepared for passengers was starboard side No. 9, but for reasons never properly explained, the boarding of passengers was delayed. First Class Steward Edward Wheelton and Saloon Steward William Ward both testified that they saw Officer Murdoch and Bruce Ismay helping prepare the boat.

Once Bruce could be of no further assistance at lifeboat No. 9, he progressed to lifeboats 11, 13 and 15, only to find that preparations were already well underway. It was intended that these three starboard lifeboats were to be lowered to 'A' deck, immediately below the Boat Deck.

While Bruce was in the vicinity of No. 9 boat, First Class passenger 22-year-old Edith Rosenbaum arrived on the Boat Deck just as the three boats were being lowered. Bruce Ismay noticed her and was surprised by her presence. Ismay led her to a nearby staircase leading directly to 'A' deck below, where she was quickly helped into lifeboat No. 11. Twenty-two years later, while writing her memoirs, she recalled her chance meeting with Bruce:

> I went out on the boat deck and stood in a direct line of sight with Mr. Bruce Ismay. He called out, 'What are you doing on this boat? I thought all women had already left' and he cried out, 'If there are any women around, come over to this staircase at once'. I walked over to Mr Ismay who pushed me swiftly down the narrow iron staircase.

As there was nothing more he could do to assist with the starboard lifeboats, Bruce hurried over to the port side, first arriving at aft lifeboat No. 16, where he met First Class Stewardess Evelyn Marsden. During her youth, Australian-born Miss Marsden was instructed in horse riding and rowing, the latter being a skill which would now be instrumental in helping to save her own life, along with many others. Evelyn had qualified as a nurse and worked in Melbourne hospitals, but although she enjoyed her profession, she was eventually driven by her spirit of adventure and love for the sea.

She decided to board the White Star liner *Persic* and headed for her parents' homeland, England. While there, Evelyn signed on as part of the crew of *Titanic*'s slightly older sister, *Olympic*. She officially signed on as First Class stewardess, utilising her nursing skills if needed. It was probably while she was aboard *Olympic* that she met William Abel James, working as a ship's doctor. The couple fell in love immediately.

Miss Marsden and William James became engaged soon afterwards, making plans to marry later that year. The young couple transferred to *Titanic* for her maiden voyage, retaining the duties they held aboard *Olympic*. Owing to a last-minute change, William was transferred to another vessel, leaving 28-year-old Miss Marsden to travel without him.

Bruce Ismay quickly realised Miss Marsden was reluctant to climb aboard lifeboat No. 16. As she was a stewardess, Evelyn felt that she had no place in a lifeboat until all passengers had left. Bruce suggested to Miss Marsden that she should climb aboard the lifeboat, saying to her, 'You are all women now'. Once lowered to the water, Miss Marsden assisted in rowing the boat away from the danger of the sinking vessel, continuing to row until she boarded the rescue ship *Carpathia*. Once back in England, Evelyn eagerly awaited the return of her fiancé, finally joining him in matrimony on 24 July 1912.

Little is known of Miss Marsden's encounter with Bruce as she was not required to give evidence at either the British or American inquiries. However, this letter sent to Ismay by Marsden's new husband, three months after the *Titanic* disaster, clearly demonstrates how Bruce was instrumental in persuading her to board the lifeboat:

Poste Restante
General post office
London
29th July 1912

Bruce Ismay Esq.

Dear Sir,
    I had wished to write to you before this but now I have to; for I wish to ask your influence on my behalf.

I was married on Wednesday last 24 July, and to you I feel so unspeakably, undyingly grateful, for as she says, had it not been for you, she would not have been alive, and so my wife today – words, and words written are very cold, Sir – but do believe me, when I say how utterly grateful I am to you for saving her life. She was a stewardess, only a stewardess, but that made no difference to you. And so you saved her, and I am happy to have made her my wife as soon as I returned to England. She is Australian, a nurse qualified at the Adelaide General Hospital. I am wishful to take her back to Australia and make a home for her out there and so I ask your favour, that you will allow me to work my passage out to Australia as Surgeon on one of your ships, and also that you will allow her to accompany me. I have saved enough money to pay her passage.

I called today at your London Office and was instructed to call again on Wednesday. In the meantime I am making my appeal to you.

Well Sir, whether you grant it or not, I shall get to Australia somehow or other. I cannot tell you how I thank you. She never ceases to sing your praises, and so from two hearts there will daily come a prayer for 'Bruce Ismay' this, as you said 'you are all women now' and she and I sincerely say 'Dieu vous benisse' [God bless you]

Yours ever gratefully,

W.A. James

Although Bruce did reply to Dr James' letter, the wording of Bruce's reply is unknown. However, records show the couple arrived at Semaphore Anchorage, Adelaide, in November 1912, aboard *Irishman*, a steamer operated by the White Star-Dominion Line. Evelyn was listed as matron, with her husband listed as ship's doctor. Therefore, it can be inferred that Bruce

Ismay had arranged for both Mr and Mrs James to work their passage to Australia.

Going back to *Titanic's* Boat Deck – Bruce left the vicinity of lifeboat No. 16 and moved along the port side of the Boat Deck, eventually reaching emergency lifeboat No. 2. There he met a small group of First Class female passengers who were refusing to board the lifeboat. Recognising their anxiety, Bruce escorted them over to the starboard side in the expectation that there would be one or two lifeboats remaining. Bruce had known that the majority of starboard lifeboats had already been lowered, and therefore he felt that the situation would be much calmer on that side of the ship.

During the fifth day of the British *Titanic* inquiry, while being questioned by Mr Harbison, Night Watchman James Johnson recalled, 'Mr Ismay tried to walk round and get a lot of women to come to our boat [No. 2]. He took them across to the starboard side.' Later, while being questioned by Mr Cotter, Johnson said, 'I saw Mr Ismay try to drive a few, and he had a pair of slippers on and his dust coat, and he was trying to get the women, and they would not go in for him into our boat.'

Bruce, along with his group of women, arrived at Collapsible C, which was located between a set of chocks on the forward part of the Boat Deck. The lifeboat's canvas sides had already been raised and the boat fitted to the now vacant davits of emergency lifeboat No. 1.

There is some evidence of an incident immediately prior to Ismay's arrival at Collapsible C. During the American inquiry First Class passenger Hugh Woolner told Senator Smith about a commotion which drew him toward the collapsible boat, and how he saw two flashes of a pistol. Woolner described how he and Mauritz Steffansson 'helped clear that boat of the men who were climbing in, because there was a bunch of women – I think Italians and foreigners – who were standing on the outside of the crowd, unable to make their way toward the side of the boat'. The men whom Woolner described quickly made their way to the port side of the ship. On arrival, Ismay once again assisted in loading this lifeboat, the ninth and last to be successfully lowered from the starboard side.

This was the lifeboat in which Bruce left the stricken vessel, the repercussions of which would stay with him for the remainder of his life. The circumstances in which Bruce Ismay boarded lifeboat Collapsible C were the subject of much debate, a debate which continues to this day.

During the American inquiry into the *Titanic* disaster, Quartermaster George Rowe was questioned by Senator Burton. Rowe told the inquiry, 'The order was given to lower the boat. The chief officer wanted to know if there were more women and children. There were none in the vicinity. Two gentlemen passengers got in; the boat was then lowered.'

At the British inquiry, Second Class Steward Edward Brown gave a very different account of the circumstances in which Ismay boarded the lifeboat. Mr Butler Aspinall asked Brown if Bruce Ismay had been taking any part in connection with lifeboat C. Brown replied, 'Yes, he was calling out for the women and children first. He helped to get them into that boat and he went into it himself to receive the women and children.' Later, while being examined by Mr Cotter, Edward Brown reasserted his previous statement. Mr Cotter wished to verify that Brown had witnessed Bruce standing in the lifeboat, Brown replied, 'He was receiving women and children in the collapsible boat when it was hanging over the side on the davits.'

During the seventh day of the British inquiry, while being questioned by Sir Robert Finlay, Mr Ismay suggested that his recollection was different to that of Mr Brown. Bruce recalled that he was helping women and children into the lifeboat while on the Boat Deck, not from within the lifeboat. According to Ismay, he only entered the lifeboat at the very last moment, as the boat was leaving, and that he could see no women or children in the vicinity.

On the fifth day of the American inquiry, another account was given by Second Officer Lightoller. When examined by Senator Smith, Lightoller made the following statement:

> Chief Officer Wilde was at the starboard collapsible boat in which Mr Ismay went away, and that he told Mr Ismay, 'There are no more women on board the ship.' Wilde was a pretty big, powerful chap, and he was a man that would not argue very long. Mr Ismay was right there. Naturally he was there close to the boat, because he was working at the boats and he had been working at the collapsible boat, and that is why he was there, and Mr Wilde, who was near him, simply bundled him into the boat.

There may be a tantalising clue suggesting that until Collapsible C was being lowered, Ismay had no intention of leaving the ship. This may be speculated by the fact that he helped with many lifeboats before his last-moment departure, together with the lack of any evidence that he ever wore a life preserver. Multiple witnesses who saw Bruce on the Boat Deck describe him as only wearing pyjamas, slippers and an overcoat.

The details surrounding Bruce Ismay's escape from *Titanic* may never be accurately established, but there is little doubt that from the moment he stepped into the lifeboat, his life would be changed forever.

Once Collapsible C had been lowered into the water, Bruce took his turn to assist with rowing, seated with his back to the ship. Some say he could not bear to turn around and see the once-marvelled ship being devoured by the icy sea, while others say that he dared not see the fate of the passengers and crew left behind. Although it may never be ascertained whether either of these contentions are true, one thing is abundantly clear – in order for Bruce to have turned around, he would have almost certainly broken off from rowing, thereby disrupting the cadence of the remaining oarsmen.

9

CARPATHIA RESCUE AND BRUCE'S HOMECOMING

Many of the passengers aboard *Titanic*'s lifeboats, some barely alive, were aware that Cunard Line's *Carpathia* had answered *Titanic*'s distress calls and was steaming toward them at full speed. Under the command of Captain Rostron, the ship had been racing toward *Titanic*'s last reported position since *Titanic*'s 12.15 a.m. distress call had been received.

Despite the best efforts of *Carpathia*'s crew, the ship arrived approximately one and a half hours after *Titanic* slipped beneath the icy water, taking with her just over 1,500 lives. Given that *Titanic*'s reported position was inaccurate by about 12 nautical miles, it was only by good fortune that one of the crew members had seen a light on the horizon as a distress flare was fired. It is most likely that the flare was fired by Officer Boxhall who was in charge of port-side lifeboat No. 2. Being alerted by the flare, *Carpathia* first arrived at this lifeboat, which became the first to be rescued, with boat No. 12 being the last lifeboat to be recovered four hours later.

Collapsible C, the lifeboat in which Bruce Ismay was present, was among the last lifeboats to be taken on board *Carpathia*. Bruce Ismay was able to climb aboard *Carpathia* using a Jacob's ladder. Once on board, as with all other survivors, he was offered a hot drink and soup, which he repeatedly refused. Observations of Bruce made by several passengers and crew members suggested that Bruce did not appear to be in complete control of his state of mind, and this was also recognised by *Carpathia*'s doctor, who quickly ushered Bruce to his own cabin.

Bruce had taken a place in the lifeboat when he thought that all the women had left the ship. When he heard that there were still some left aboard, he became inconsolable. To make matters worse, he had just learned that his butler, Richard Fry, who had accompanied him as his valet, and his secretary, Harrison, were also missing. He had not seen either of them after the collision as he had been on the Boat Deck helping to load the lifeboats. He felt that he was responsible for their presence on the ship and consequently their loss. When he finally returned to England, one of the first things he did was to ensure that their widows would receive a generous lifetime annuity.

While aboard *Carpathia*, Bruce was heavily criticised by some of the survivors – he had the comfort of the doctor's cabin, while others had only a blanket. Two weeks later, at the American inquiry, Senator Smith asked Ismay a forthright question regarding his accommodation on *Carpathia*. Smith asked Ismay, 'Not desiring to be impertinent at all, but in order that I may not be charged with omitting to do my duty, I would like to know where you went after you boarded the *Carpathia*, and how you happened to go there?'

Ismay's reply was equally forthright:

Mr Chairman, I understand that my behaviour on board the *Titanic*, and subsequently on board the *Carpathia* has been very severely criticised. I want to court the fullest inquiry, and I place myself unreservedly in the hands of yourself and any of your colleagues, to ask me any questions in regard to my conduct; so please do not hesitate to do so and I will answer them to the best of my ability. So far as the *Carpathia* is concerned, Sir, when I got on board the ship I stood up with my back against the bulkhead, and somebody came up to me and said, 'Will you not go into the saloon and get some soup, or something to drink?' 'No,' I said, 'I really do not want anything at all.' He said, 'Do go and get something.' I said, 'No; if you will leave me alone I will be very much happier here.' I said, 'If you will get me in some room where I can be quiet, I wish you would.' He said, 'Please go in the saloon and get something hot.' I said, 'I would rather not.' Then he took me and put me into a room. I did not know whose room it was, at all. This man proved to be Frank McGee, doctor of the *Carpathia*. I was in that room until I left the ship. I was never outside the door of that room. During the whole of the time I was in this room, I never had anything of a solid nature, at all; I lived on soup. I did not want very much of anything. The room was constantly being entered by people asking for the doctor. The doctor did not sleep in the room the first night. The doctor slept in the room the other nights that I was on board that ship. Mr. Jack Thayer was brought into the room the morning we got on board the *Carpathia*. He stayed in the room for some little time, and the doctor came in after he had been in, I should think, about a quarter of an hour, and he said to this young boy, 'Would you not like something to eat?' He said, 'I would like some bacon and eggs' which he had. The doctor did not have a suite of rooms on the ship. He simply had this one small room, which he himself occupied and dressed in every night and morning.

John Jack Thayer was the 17-year-old son of First Class passenger John Thayer II, a director and a second vice president of the Pennsylvania Railroad Company. The Thayer family were acquainted with Bruce Ismay, and it was perhaps because of this familiarity that the doctor had asked young Thayer to visit Ismay, in the hope that this would help relieve his terribly nervous condition, with the expectation that Jack could persuade Bruce to talk.

The young Thayer later wrote about visiting Bruce Ismay:

> I immediately went down and as there was no answer to my knock, I went right in. He was seated, in his pyjamas, on his bunk, staring straight ahead, shaking all over, like a leaf.
>
> My entrance apparently did not dawn on his consciousness. Even when I spoke to him and tried to engage him in conversation, telling him he had a perfect right to take the last boat, he paid absolutely no attention and continued to look ahead, with a fixed stare.
>
> I am almost certain that on the Titanic his hair had been black with slight tinges of grey, but his hair was now virtually snow white.
>
> I have never seen a man so completely wrecked. Nothing I could do or say brought any response.
>
> As I closed the door he was still looking fixedly ahead.[1]

By the way in which Bruce has been described while on board *Carpathia*, and possibly during the American inquiry, it may well be that by today's medical standards, Bruce could have been described as suffering from what is known today as Post-Traumatic Stress Disorder, at least for a short while, however, PTSD did not become officially recognised until several decades later.

The fixed stare which Jack Thayer spoke about may also be connected with the suggestion that *Carpathia*'s doctor had administered an opiate, possibly opium or laudanum. This was mentioned in a telegram sent by *Carpathia*'s Captain Rostron. Although the opiate's effect on Bruce's state of mind is not known, it is interesting that Officer Lightoller, *Titanic*'s senior surviving officer, persuaded Bruce Ismay to issue instructions for *Titanic*'s surviving crew to be returned to England at the earliest possible moment. Consequently, a message to this effect was sent to the White Star Liner *Cedric*, which was berthed in New York, about to sail for England.

During the fifth day of the subsequent American inquiry, while being questioned by Senator Burton, Officer Lightoller stated:

Previous to having the conversation with Mr Ismay in regard to any telegrams that were sent to our office in New York with reference to holding the Cedric, the other three officers and myself had spoken about it casually, saying we knew the Cedric and we thought it a jolly good idea if we could get home with her if we were in time to catch her. We were very much disappointed at the delay through fog. We were saying all the time, 'It is a great pity if we will miss the Cedric. If we could only get home in time to get everybody on board the Cedric, we shall probably be able to keep the men together as much as possible.' Otherwise, you understand, once the men get in New York, naturally these men are not going to hang around New York or hang around anywhere else. They want to get to sea to earn money to keep their wives and families, and they would ship off. You cannot find a sailor but what will ship off at once if he gets the opportunity. They simply would stand this off as a loss or stand it off as a bad debt, and probably try to ship off somewhere. In a case like this, where the men are brought into prominence, they are very frequently offered berths immediately. Certain of the steerage passengers were offered berths by the saloon passengers. They were offered berths to go and be servants, or whatever it was until they found employment.

Our crew would in all probability have done the same, and we would have lost a number of them, probably some very important witnesses. They would perhaps ship on some yacht, which very often they do. A great many of them, quarter-masters especially, ship on gentlemen's yachts in New York, because they know they are thoroughly capable men. They are just as good men as they can obtain in the world, and there is great demand for them; much to our regret, because we lose them.

On having a conversation with Mr Ismay he also mentioned about the Cedric and asked me my opinion about it, and I frankly stated that it was the best thing in the world to do if we could catch the Cedric.

Later on he remarked that owing to weather conditions it was very doubtful if we would catch the Cedric. I said, 'Yes; it is doubtful. It will be a great pity if she sails without us.' 'Do you think it will be advisable to hold her up?' I said, 'Most undoubtedly; the best thing in the world to hold her up.'

A telegram was dispatched asking them to hold the Cedric until we got in, to which we received the reply that it was not advisable to hold the Cedric. He asked what I thought about it. I said, 'I think we ought to hold her, and you ought to telegraph and insist on their holding her and preventing the crew getting around in New York.' We discussed the pros and cons and deemed it advisable to keep the crew together as much as we could, so we could get home, and we might then be able to choose our important witnesses and let the remainder go to sea and earn money for themselves. So I believe the other telegram was sent.

I may say that at that time Mr Ismay did not seem to me to be in a mental condition to finally decide anything. I tried my utmost to rouse Mr Ismay, for he was obsessed with the idea, and kept repeating, that he ought to have gone down with the ship because he found that women had gone down. I told him there was no such reason; I told him a very great deal; I tried to get that idea out of his head, but he was taken with it; and I know the doctor tried too; but we had difficulty in arousing Mr Ismay, purely owing to that wholly and solely, that women had gone down in the boat and he had not. You can call the doctor of the Carpathia, and he will verify that statement.

By the time *Carpathia* arrived in New York, the liner *Cedric* had already left for England. Bruce's wife Florence, sorrowful for the huge loss of life but also delighted by the news of her husband's survival, had been making plans to leave for New York to be with her husband. Philip Franklin, vice president of IMM, advised Florence of Bruce's intention to leave immediately for England, and therefore the decision was made that she should wait for his return.

Meanwhile, as *Carpathia* was heading towards New York, Senator William Alden Smith had been arranging for an inquiry to take place once the ship arrived. Fearful that Ismay, along with *Titanic* crew members would make their way to England, he arranged a naval escort for *Carpathia* to ensure no one left the ship before it docked.

Various details of the *Titanic* disaster were beginning to reach the world's press, gaining particular attention from the newspapers owned by William Randolph Hearst, a one-time friend of Bruce Ismay. A disagreement between the two men some twenty years earlier had left the friendship scarred, with Hearst harbouring much ill-feeling toward Bruce. Although the world's newspapers were reporting on the *Titanic* disaster; it was mainly those owned by Hearst that were responsible for launching the most vicious campaigns against Ismay and the White Star Line.

Carpathia arrived in New York on the evening of 18 April, where a large crowd had assembled, many seeking news of their loved ones. There was also a large assembly of doctors, nurses and clergy, as well as a delegation from the Salvation Army whose aim was to care mostly for the steerage passengers. Soon after *Carpathia* docked, Ismay was visited by Philip Franklin, followed soon afterwards by Senator William Smith.

The purpose of Senator Smith's visit was to officially inform Bruce Ismay that he would be required to appear before the forthcoming Senate inquiry, which was due to begin the following day. Subsequently, Bruce, along with surviving crew members were immediately summoned to appear before the American Senate Committee, thereby confining them to American shores until 30 April. Beginning in New York, the inquiry relocated to Washington DC, later returning to New York. The same day that the inquiry ended in Washington, Senator Smith received a letter from Bruce Ismay:

Washington, D.C., April 25, 1912.
Hon. William Alden Smith,
Chairman, etc., Washington, D.C.

Sir: On learning of the appointment of the committee of inquiry after the arrival of the steamship Carpathia last Thursday night in New York, the members of the committee who met me at the steamer will doubtless recall that personally, and as managing director of the White Star Line, I welcomed this inquiry and though under severe mental and physical strain as a result of the disaster placed myself voluntarily at the disposal of your committee, and expressed the utmost willingness to give them all information in my possession to the best of my ability.

I voluntarily appeared before the committee the following day, Friday, April 19, and, though not in the best of condition to give evidence, I testified at length regarding all matters connected with the accident and offered to produce or have produced before the committee any officers or persons from our technical department, or from the technical department of Harland & Wolff, the builders, that might be thought necessary or desirable in order to enable the committee to investigate this tragic occurrence in the most complete manner.

I have regularly attended every hearing of the committee held in New York and in Washington daily since my first examination, on April 19, and have held myself in readiness continuously to answer the call of the committee to give any further testimony that might be desired, though personally I do not see that I can be of any further assistance to the committee. If, however, after the production of the technical or other evidence, the committee is of the opinion that I can help its deliberations in any manner, I shall hold myself in readiness to answer its further call, upon reasonable notice from the committee.

I am hopeful that the committee may be able to suggest ways and means for the avoidance of similar accidents in the future, and anything that I personally or that the company with which I am connected can do to further that object will be gladly done.

If the committee wishes to examine me further at the present time I hope it may be found convenient to do so promptly in order that I may go home to my family. In view of my experience at the time of the disaster and subsequently,

I hope that the committee will feel that this request is not unreasonable.

The committee is also aware that an inquiry into this disaster has been started by my own Government, which has jurisdiction to deal with matters of serious importance to the interests of the company, which I understand are outside the scope of the present inquiry, and which urgently require my personal attention in England.

In these circumstances I respectfully request that if the committee wishes to examine me further it will be good enough to do so at the earliest practical moment, and excuse me from further attendance at the present time.

Respectfully,

Bruce Ismay[2]

On receipt of Bruce's letter, Senator Smith quickly sent his very direct reply:

Washington, D.C., April 25, 1912.
Mr. J. Bruce Ismay,
Willard Hotel, Washington, D.C.

Sir: Replying to your letter of this date, just received, permit me to say that I am not unmindful of the fact that you are being detained in this country against your will, and, probably, at no little inconvenience to yourself and family. I can readily see that your absence from England at a time so momentous in the affairs of your company would be most embarrassing, but the horror of the Titanic catastrophe and its importance to the people of the world call for scrupulous investigation into the causes leading up to the disaster, that future losses of similar character may, if possible, be avoided. To that end, we have been charged by the Senate of the

United States with the duty of making this official inquiry, and, so far as I am concerned, nothing will be left undone which may in any manner contribute to this end. As I said to you in New York on Friday evening last, when you asked to be permitted to return home, and again on Saturday night, when you made the same request, I shall not consent to your leaving this country until the fullest inquiry has been made into the circumstances surrounding the accident. This information can be fully detailed by yourself and other officers of your company and the officers and crew of your ship. I am working night and day to achieve this result, and you should continue to help me instead of annoying me and delaying my work by your personal importunities.

Trusting you will receive this letter in the spirit in which it is written, I am,

Very respectfully,

W.M. Alden Smith,

Chairman Senate Subcommittee Investigating the Titanic Disaster.[3]

All those summoned to testify were keen to return home at the earliest possible moment, consequently, at noon on 2 May 1912, Bruce, along with four surviving officers, Frederick Fleet and about forty other crew members left for England aboard the White Star liner *Adriatic*.

It had been arranged that Bruce's wife Florence would travel to Queenstown, Ireland, where she boarded *Adriatic*, enabling her to travel the remainder of the journey to Liverpool with her beloved husband, finally returning to England's shores on 11 May.

While Bruce was leaving New York, the British inquiry, known as the British Wreck Commissioners Inquiry, was just beginning in London. Headed by John Bigham, Lord Mersey, the inquiry would last for two months, with Bruce Ismay being sworn in seven days after returning to England.

Both the British and American inquiries cleared Bruce Ismay of any blame. Many American citizens, and to some extent the British too, were guided only by sensationalist newspaper reports that focused on Ismay's actions while aboard *Titanic*, with many seeing it as a trial by media.

Despite his dislike for the press, Bruce had a letter drafted to *The Times* newspaper, wishing to address the issue of *Titanic's* speed:

DRAFT

To the editor of 'The Times.' [Undated]

Dear Sir,

So much has been said in America, and also to some extent in this country, to the effect that Mr. Ismay was responsible for the speed at which "Titanic" was going at the time of accident, and that his presence on board would be an incentive to Captain Smith to get the best out of the ship, that I feel I am only doing justice to him in stating what his views are in regard to speed.

When the Olympic was put into commission it was well known that under normal conditions, when on the short track, she had sufficient speed to enable her to land her passengers in New York on Tuesday afternoon, but in spite of this, Mr. Ismay laid it down that she was not to arrive there before Wednesday morning, as he preferred that the Olympic should gain in reputation for regularity of arrival rather than for speed.

In this policy he was opposed by some of his colleagues, who held the view, that the speed of Olympic should be utilised to the best advantage, that it was sacrificing her popularity not to do so, and that when all the conditions were favourable she should arrive in New York on Tuesday afternoon when on the short track, and under some pressure he deferred to their views and the instruction not to arrive before Wednesday morning was withdrawn.

The Olympic made three voyages to New York before the restriction as to the day of arrival was withdrawn.

The instruction given to "Titanic" before leaving Queenstown was that she was not to arrive at the Ambrose Lightship (23 miles before New York) before 5 a.m. on Wednesday morning.

I think this clearly shows that Mr. Ismay is not an advocate for speed; on the contrary, his preference is for regularity of arrival at the expense of speed, and Captain Smith well knowing his views in regard to this question could not have been influenced by his presence on board.

Yours truly,

Director and Manager White Star Line

On learning of Bruce's intentions, Harold Sanderson, along with Bruce Ismay's lawyer, attempted to dissuade Ismay from taking this course of action. The day after the British inquiry concluded Sanderson sent a letter requesting Bruce to reconsider his plans to write to the press. An extract from this letter shows that Sanderson was clearly not in favour of Ismay's intention:

4 July 12

My dear Bruce,

I shall be interested to learn what decision you come to, as to communicating with the press, but for what it may be worth I offer my advice, which is to do nothing.

This prompted a reply that Bruce sent to Harold the following day, clearly demonstrating the difficult position in which Bruce felt he had been placed:

5th July 1912

I have not yet decided what I am going to do in regard to communicating with the press and am much obliged for your advice, which is to do nothing.

I am afraid we look at the position from entirely different points of view: you have not been attacked, whereas I have, so you can easily afford to sit and do nothing.

I certainly feel that the result of the trial has been to exonerate me entirely of having taken any part in the navigation of the ship, but what I am very much afraid of is that Lord Mersey in his finding will make absolutely no mention of this point, as it is outside the terms of his reference.

It is not my intention to do anything in a hurry, or without mature consideration, and under lawyer's advice, but at present my inclination is to take steps to let the public know what Lord Mersey's views are in regard to myself, which they do not now know, as it has only come out in the evidence, and has not been reported to the press.

Almost three weeks later, while waiting for the British Wreck Commissioners Report to be released, Bruce's lawyer, Mr F.M. Radcliffe, also wrote an interesting letter:

Queen Insurance Buildings,
10, Dale Street,
Liverpool,
23rd July 1912.

Telegraphic Address
'Ayrecliff', Liverpool
Tel No. 1066.

Dear Mr. Ismay,

I thought the proposal of writing to the Times was not
to be considered unless some necessity seemed to arise out
of Lord Mersey's Judgment or, at any rate until after that
Judgment. I imagine this is still your view, and I decidedly
concur in its wisdom.

It seems to me impossible to say beforehand what should
or should not be written in view of the Judgment – that
must depend on its contents. You may say that, whatever
the Judgment contains, it will not contain an explanation
as to your views on the question of speed, and that you
are entitled, under the special circumstances, to be relieved
of the suggestion that you are in general an advocate of
high speeds. I should be surprised if you do not find in
Lord Mersey's Judgment a statement that he concurs in the
statement of Sir Rufus Isaacs on p. 901 that the White Star
Line have 'proved conclusively' that they did not desire to
make a record passage; that what they did intend to do was
to arrive on the Wednesday morning at 5 o'clock 'which
would by no means have been a record passage; and that
certainly it was not necessary to push this vessel at its
extreme speed in order to do that'. A more complete vindication from a charge of ordering or influencing excessive
speed I cannot imagine; and if the Judgment contains this,
or anything like it, it would be a mistake to write a letter
which is not only unnecessary, but which at best, could
only show that you at first opposed a Tuesday arrival for
the Olympic, but yielded to that policy at the suggestion of
your colleagues.

But, as I said before, the proper course is to see what the Judgment in fact says before deciding anything.

Yours very sincerely,

F.M. Radcliffe.

The day after the official report was released, and while waiting to receive his copy of this report, Radcliffe followed up with another letter:

Queen Insurance Buildings,
10, Dale Street,
Liverpool.
August 1912

Telegraphic Address:
'Ayrcliff', Liverpool.
Tel No. 1066

Dear Mr. Ismay,

The official print of Lord Mersey's Judgment has not yet arrived, but I have read it carefully as printed in various newspapers.

It seems to me to afford you complete exoneration from the charge or suggestion that you were responsible for the speed of the 'Titanic' at the time of the disaster. Moreover, Lord Mersey expressly refers to the suggestion that your presence on board might have induced the Captain to neglect precautions which he would otherwise have taken, and expressly finds to the contrary 'The evidence shows that the Captain was not trying to make any record passage, or indeed any exceptional quick passage. He was not trying to please anybody, but was exercising his own discretion in the way he thought best'. It seems to me that nothing can be usefully added to this.

You may say that the phrase 'was not trying to please anybody' leaves it to be supposed that the Captain might have thought that going at full speed would please you; and you would like it to be stated that you had no reason for such an opinion, but the contrary. In my judgement this is a point which you would be very ill-advised to labour, for many reasons.

1) The Judgment is entirely in your favour on this point as it stands and I do not think it is open to that interpretation suggested.

2) This is shown by the tone of the whole of the press, none of whom differ from this part of the Judgment.

3) To begin to supplement the Judgment or dot its i's, cross its t's, would only be to invite a correspondence in the papers, or in other words, to put out your head to be hit.

4) Moreover, while the question of the speed of the 'Olympic', and the General policy of your line as to speed might usefully have been referred to in evidence, I am strongly of opinion that the incident of the 'Olympic' has a double edge. If you seek to use it as showing that you personally do not press for high speed, you must not be surprised if other people use it as showing that you are prepared to acquiesce in a speed higher than you yourself think necessary when others press for it for business reasons, and since the determining voice is yours, as Chairman, the responsibility is yours. Captain Smith was Captain of the 'Olympic' as well as the 'Titanic'. There is no evidence that he knew of the differences in the office on this question or of your individual views; but if he did, he knew equally that you waived those views. I know all that is to be said on the other side; but I think, if you start a correspondence, you would be giving any ill-disposed person pellets to fire at you, on such a doubtful basis; and

I think you may well be content with the very clear finding of Lord Mersey on the matter.

5) You have taken the whole affair calmly and with dignity.
Do nothing to lead people to suppose that you are
not satisfied with a vindication which is recognised to
be complete.

The only dissentient note is the ill-natured phrase in the
leading article of the 'Daily Mail', obviously directed only
to the incident of the boats. As I told you at the beginning,
different people till the end of time will take different views
on ethical questions. That you should have one dissentient
voice only in all the respectable newspapers of England, is
an extraordinary evidence of the fact that public opinion
is on your side on the question of your leaving the vessel,
and I have only heard the Daily Mail article mentioned to
be disapproved.

I suppose that when a good man is charged with an offence
in a criminal court the verdict 'not guilty' always sounds
a little cold to his friends. They would like something very
much warmer – something which would embody their
knowledge that not only was he not guilty, but could not have
been guilty. That is not the way of the world. One has to think
what it would have meant had the fallibility of human minds
committed the monstrous injustice of bringing in an opposite
verdict (as has happened before now) and be grateful.

I can heartily and sincerely congratulate you on the ter-
mination of a long period of suspense, and on the Judgment
and on the attitude of the press. In my opinion the proper
course is to regard the Judgment, with its complete exoneration of yourself from blame, as pronouncing the last word
on the matter.

Yours very sincerely,

F.M. Radcliffe

As Lord Mersey's final report was about to be released, Bruce received another letter of encouragement from his friend and colleague, Harold Sanderson:

24 June 1912

My dear Bruce,

   The office has kept me posted concerning what has been passing between you concerning the 'Titanic' Inquiry & I feel sure that the wisest course is now to do nothing more, but to leave it to counsel to put the case in all its hearings, both from the personal and business point of view, fairly before the court, to await the finding, which I am very hopeful will not be worse than to credit Capt. Smith with an error of judgement in the matter of speed, & I would not now be surprised if he even escaped that. As to yourself I feel confident the allusion to yourself which will be made by Lord Mersey will set your mind at peace. In the meanwhile my dear Bruce, try to see things as they really are, not through glasses of a morbid tint.

Due to the lack of agreement from his colleagues, the release of Lord Mersey's final report, and under the advice of his lawyer, Bruce's statement was never released to the press.

To date, the author of this book has found no evidence proving that Bruce's instruction had been transmitted to the commander of *Titanic*. Furthermore, Bruce's statement was unlikely to have stood up to scrutiny as *Olympic*'s documented New York arrivals did not support this notion.

10

Bruce Ismay's Retirement from International Mercantile Marine

Once both the American and British inquiries were over Bruce once again began to focus on thoughts of his retirement. In November 1911, Bruce had advised Harold Sanderson that he was considering appointing him as chairman of the Shaw Savill & Albion Company, a shipping company that had become woven into the Oceanic Steam Navigation Company. This prompted Sanderson to send a private communication to Bruce in which he explained that he too was set to retire from IMM, much earlier than initially anticipated. This letter would, in turn, set a chain of events in the lead-up to Ismay's retirement, an extract of which appears below:

18th November 1911

My dear Bruce,
    You are, of course, aware that I have had it in mind for some time to retire from the position that I hold in Liverpool, and

that when we were last in New York together, the period of my remaining service was referred to as of two or three years' duration, and this fact has at least once been mentioned in conversation between us since that time.

It was my intention, after the turn of the New Year, to intimate to you that I would like this period to expire with the next calendar year, 1912, but I feel that the Shaw Savill matter places an obligation upon me to disclose to you at once what I have in mind, for I realise, of course, that the knowledge of my approaching withdrawal might very reasonably cause your views to alter, as to my taking on the chairmanship, either temporarily or permanently, and I have, therefore, kept the matter quite open and subject to further review by your good self.

I will not attempt to disguise the fact that having been identified with the White Star Line so long and so intimately, the prospect of terminating the connection causes me real distress, and I dislike to think of it; but, on the other hand, the strain of the Liverpool work is, I know, beginning to tell on me, and I want to arrange the remainder of my business career in a manner that will extend it as long as is possible and desirable, and it is not practicable to do so without asking to be relieved of my Liverpool work. We have good, loyal, able men under us, who, I am convinced will rise to the occasion if you will increase their responsibilities, and I most earnestly hope that, upon reflection, you will not harbour the thought that I am, in any sense, deserting the ship prematurely, or that I am doing what is not right and fair by you and the company. That would not be doing me justice, I honestly believe, and were you to do so, it would cause me more unhappiness than I could possibly express in words.

Our friends in New York will not be surprised to learn of my intention to retire, as it was referred to at an interview which I had with Grenfell, on their behalf, in New York on the occasion already referred to, when you and I discussed the same subject, and I would like the fact to be communicated to them by your good self, as I feel that to be in every way the proper procedure. It only remains for me, consequently, to place the whole matter unreservedly in your hands, and to ask you and them to accept the assurance of my very great anxiety to so arrange matters that when my connection with the company ceases on the 31st December, 1912, I may leave with the knowledge that I do so with that goodwill and regard which I have consistently sought to deserve at your and their hands.

While waiting to travel to New York aboard *Olympic*, Bruce wrote his reply to Sanderson:

Southampton
January 10th 1912

My dear Harold,
    I had a long and friendly talk with Grenfell last night, in regard to the wish you have expressed of retiring from the service of the I.M.M. Company at the end of the present year.
    During our conversation, I told him briefly of what took place when you and I talked the situation over the other day in Liverpool, referring more particularly to your remark that during the whole of your business-career you had never filled the premier position in the business in which you were engaged, and that this had caused you a certain sense of disappointment, and both Grenfell and I fully appreciate and realise your feeling.
    I further stated that, had I left the I.M.M. Company a few years ago, as I had intended, you would have taken the

position of President for a certain length of time, when you would have retired, having occupied the highest position in the service.

I repeated to Grenfell what I told you at our interview, namely, that I was prepared to resign the position of President at once in your favour, but that this apparently did not appeal to you.

I am very anxious to meet your wishes, and will gladly do anything in my power to enable you to complete your business career at the top of the tree, and, with this in view, I would ask you to seriously consider the following proposition, namely, that I will remain on as President of the I.M.M. Company until the 31st December, 1912 during which period I would practically make London my headquarters coming to Liverpool, say, once a week, in order to attend to my duties as director of the Liverpool, London & Globe, the Sea Insurance Company, and the Protection Association, and you should take entire charge of and be responsible for the conduct of the Liverpool business, only referring to me matters of exceptional importance, and questions of policy; that you should take the chairmanship of Shaw, Savill & Albion Company and continue looking after the London business as you have done in the past.

My being away from Liverpool, and your duties in London necessitating your being there to a certain extent, would throw more responsibility on the managers in Liverpool, which would give them an opportunity of showing what was in them, and enable you to judge of their qualifications for future promotion, as I understand you feel that, given the opportunity, some of them would rise to the occasion, and would enable you to decide which, if any of them, is capable of succeeding you in Liverpool when the time arrived for you to fill the position as President.

On the 31st December, 1912, I would retire from the Presidency, and I hope that you would see your way to succeed me, say for one or two years, or for as long as you felt inclined to remain in the business.

So long as you retained the Presidency, I would gladly afford you every help I could and, if you so desired, would continue a member of the British Committee.

Obviously, it would be very wrong for both you and I to retire from the I.M.M. Co. at the same time, and it occurs to me that the above proposal fairly meets the situation, as it would give time for matters to develop.

Accordingly, Ismay sent copies of this letter to Edward Grenfell (chairman of IMM's British Committee) and Charles Steele, a business partner and secretary of J.P. Morgan, and a member of IMM's Executive and Finance Committee.

In reply to Ismay's letter, Sanderson sent a cablegram to New York, which was waiting for Bruce on his arrival there. In his cable, Sanderson accepted Bruce's suggestion that, subject to approval, he should replace Bruce as president of IMM and expressed his delight that Bruce had offered his assistance by remaining on the British Committee. On 18 January 1912, Bruce sent a further reply to Sanderson, which contained an interesting footnote:

At the moment, for many reasons, (which I have no doubt you will appreciate), I feel I would like to retain the Chairmanship of the White Star Line, so long as I am in any way connected with the business, but of course I could only hold this position if it was entirely agreeable to you.

The following day, Bruce sent a further letter to Sanderson in which he appears to have reconsidered his earlier thoughts of remaining chairman of the White Star Line:

January 19th, 1912

My dear Harold,

Since writing to you yesterday, I have been thinking over my suggestion that, in the event of your becoming President of the I.M.M. Co., I should retain the chairmanship of the White Star Line, and have come to the conclusion that this would not do at all. I have had a talk with Steele this afternoon, and he thinks it would be well to leave the whole matter in abeyance for the present.

Soon after arriving back in England, Bruce wrote to Harold Sanderson in the hope of satisfactorily explaining his personal point of view to him:

London, S.W. February 9th, 1912

My dear Harold,

In anticipation of the conversation we must have in reference to the matter that has recently been the subject of letter and cable correspondence between us, I think it well to put down my misunderstanding of the position, as doing so may be of assistance when we come to discuss the situation.

It is my intention (subject always to the I.M.M. not giving me six months' notice to resign the presidency at an earlier date), to remain in my present position until the 30th June, 1913 instead of resigning on the 31st December, 1912, as indicated in my letter of the 10th ultimo. My reason for this is, that, in any circumstances, I can only look upon my prospective severance from the business with which I have been connected all my career with very mixed and doubtful feelings, and, perhaps selfishly, I am anxious to make it as easy as possible, which, after all, is not unreasonable.

I feel that making such an entire change in my mode of life as that contemplated would come less hardly if made in the summer than in the winter, as in the former case, I should have good weather, long days, and my shooting to look forward to, which would give me occupation for some months and this would enable me to better prepare for the time when I should have little or nothing with which to fill up my time.

Forgive me for remarking that it is difficult to understand why you should be apparently anxious to assume the presidency on the 1st January, 1913, but doing so on the 1st July, 1913 has no attraction to you whatever. This, however, is not my business. I understand your position is as follows, viz.:-

If I remain as president of the I.M.M. Company until the 30th June, 1913 you wish to resign from all your positions on the 31st December, 1912; if on the 1st July, 1913, all being well, and you feel that the interval during which you have been out of the business is not sufficient to put you out of touch with affairs, and our friends in New York wish it, you are prepared to accept the position of president of the I.M.M. Company.

If I have accurately stated your decision, and I think I have, let us see how it would work out from a business and personal point of view. The position would be as follows:-

I would, during the last six months of office, have not the least idea as to whether or not I was going to retire from business on the 30th June, 1913, as it must be obvious that, if you decided you did not wish to assume the position of president, I must continue to do so until such time as some other arrangement could be made, as I could not, for one moment, be a party to placing the I.M.M. Company in a difficulty, and (perhaps stupidly), I feel that if both you and I were to sever our connection with the company at the same time, it would do so.

The uncertainty of what you may elect to do on the 31st July, 1913, would absolutely prevent me from making any plans for the future, as they could be dependent on your decision in regard to taking office, in fact you might determine, say in the middle of June, that you would like to do so, with the result that at two weeks' notice I should have to retire from business without having made any preparation for doing so, which I am sure you will agree is an impossible position, as there are a great many matters I would have to deal with and arrange in anticipation of any retirement and these will take time, as you will appreciate.

The very next day, Sanderson sent his reply to Bruce:

Liverpool, 10th January, '12.

My dear Bruce,

I have for years looked forward to the 31st December, 1912 as the date on which I shall take the important step of retiring, and retirement, or altered conditions, such as you propose in your letter of the 10th January would alike give me the relief and change I need. It is for the reason that I have hitherto understood that the postponement of your resignation to 30th June 1913, carried with it the obligation that I should continue for that further period, at least, in my present position, that I have said that your amended proposal had no attraction for me.

It may be seen from Bruce's reply to this letter that Sanderson's latest comments did not rest well with him. Two days after receiving Sanderson's letter, Bruce Ismay sent the following reply:

1a, Cockspur Street, London
February 14th, 1912.

I am sorry I misread your letter, but it seemed quite clear to me what you had in mind.

I understand, however, that if our banking friends will say definitely now, notwithstanding you retire from the business for six months on the 31st. December, that they would like you to take office on the 1st. July, 1913, you are prepared to accept without any qualifications whatever, from which you conclude you have no fear of losing touch of affairs during the six months you were in retirement.

Of course, I cannot express any opinion as to how your proposition will appeal to our banking friends, this is a matter for them to consider, but it occurs to me that there are many serious difficulties in the way of their coming under such a commitment.

Has it occurred to you what people will say, and think, if the suggestion you make is given effect to, viz.:- that you resign from business on the 31st December, 1912, and I resign on the 30th June, 1913, and you succeed me on the 1st July, 1913? They would, I think, naturally draw the following conclusions:-

'When Sanderson resigned, Ismay tried to carry on the business alone, failed, and had to resign, then Sanderson was brought back to take the presidency although he had resigned from the company six months previously.'

Would this not be a very natural inference to draw from what has taken place?

Please do not think I am trying to bring pressure to bear on you to remain with the company during the six months in question, as I do not wish to influence you in your decision, but no question such as that indicated in the previous paragraph would arise did you do so, and assume the office of president the day I resign without any interregnum.

I cannot help feeling that, during the conversation I hope to have with you next week, when I shall be in Liverpool, we will come to some arrangement, and I am only sorry to feel that it cannot, apparently, be one which I would permit our continuing to work together; however, in the circumstances, I suppose it cannot be helped.

As suggested, one week later, Ismay and Sanderson met in Liverpool to discuss and clarify the situation. The exchange of views resulted in agreement between the two men. Subsequently, the following memorandum was released, with copies being sent to Charles Steele and William Grenfell:

The following is the result of my conversation with Sanderson in regard to retirement, and I understand the arrangement come to is entirely satisfactory to him, viz.:-

That I should remain as president of the I.M.M. Company and hold my present position until the 30th June, 1913 on which date I resign the presidency.

Sanderson to be granted six months' leave of absence from the 31st December, 1912. During this time he would act as chairman of the Shaw, Savill, Albion Company and of George Thompson, but be entirely relieved of all other work. He wishes it understood that during this time he would receive no remuneration.

Sanderson would resume all his duties on 1st June, 1913, or some time about this date, so as to get in touch with the business, and assume the office of president of the I.M.M. Company on the 1st July, 1913.

I would continue a member of the British Committee after the 30th June, 1913, and if thought desirable, would act as a director of Shaw, Savill & Albion Company, and George Thompson & Co., either prior or subsequent to this date.

Of course, it is understood that the above arrangement has been come to subject to its being agreeable to Messrs. J.P. Morgan & Co.

[signed] Bruce Ismay
[signed] Harold H. Sanderson
London, 16th February, 1912.

Just three days later, Bruce Ismay wrote to Charles Steele to confirm his agreement to the previous letter signed by himself and Sanderson. The following is an extract of the last letter that Ismay is known to have written before the *Titanic* disaster, which referenced his retirement:

There is no reason, from my point of view, why the six months' leave of absence-should not be granted.

I am anxious that Sanderson should obtain his wish as to holding the premier position in the business in which he is engaged before he retires from business, and the only possible way of giving effect thereto is by my resigning in his favour, and this I have expressed my willingness to do.

Of course, the 30th June, 1913 is a 'far cry' and much may happen between now and then, for this reason I suggest that whatever may be arranged should be kept absolutely private until the 31st December. No good purpose would be served by making any announcement, as it would only create a feeling of unrest, and the suggested changes may never come into force.

I suggest there is no reason to come to any decision now as to the future, and we can talk the whole situation over when I see you in April.

On 2 March 1912, Charles Steele wrote his reply:

There must be something like mental telepathy in the world, for as I came down town I was thinking about the situation over there, and had just about decided to cable you making the suggestion which you had already thought of and adopted. The proposed arrangement is entirely satisfactory to me, and I hope is both to you and Sanderson. I quite agree there is no reason whatever why it should be made public at the present time, and I think it much better that nothing more should be said on the subject until the time arrives to act. I trust everything will run along smoothly now. There are lots of things that may happen before the 30th June, 1913.

With very best regards for Sanderson and yourself, believe me as ever,

Yours faithfully,

[signed] Charles Steele

Communications regarding Bruce's retirement were, for the moment, laid to rest. The company's newest liner RMS *Titanic* was nearing completion and soon to face her sea trials; neither Ismay nor Steele could have known about the events that were soon to follow.

The loss of *Titanic*, along with the ensuing American and British inquiries into the disaster and the preparations for improvements to the design and lifesaving equipment of the company's vessels, not least, the massive improvements to RMS *Olympic*, left little time for Bruce to pursue his plans for retirement. *Olympic* was taken out of service on 9 October and returned to shipbuilders Harland & Wolff, Belfast, in order to carry out the improvement work, which included the installation of extra davits to accommodate an increase in the number of lifeboats. The height of the watertight bulkheads was extended from 'E' deck to 'B' deck and a watertight inner skin was installed in the boiler and engine rooms, which created a double hull.

After *Olympic* was returned to Belfast, plans for Bruce's retirement were resumed. Although Ismay had previously arranged for Harold Sanderson to replace him as president of IMM, he had again reconsidered the question of remaining a director of the White Star Line. Deciding, along with his wife Florence, that this would be their desired course of action, he contacted the directors of IMM and Harold Sanderson to make them aware of his intentions. This prompted a letter from Edward Grenfell as follows:

PRIVATE & CONFIDENTIAL
23rd October 1912.

My dear Ismay,

Referring to your express desire to make some public announcement in the immediate future as regards your plans, I have had a talk with Mr. J.P. Morgan, Junior, and also cabled to Mr. Morgan in America in reference to our conversation of last Friday. They are both of the opinion that if a new man is to take over the presidency of the I.M.M. Company it would not be advisable for his predecessor to accept a seat on the boards of the operating companies.

As president you have been in absolute control of all the companies forming the I.M.M. Company, and you have, as was only natural, by your ability and strong personality overshadowed the other managers, and to a certain extent they have looked to you for guidance in all matters great and small. On your retirement several of these junior men will have to be promoted to more responsible positions, and I think it will be easier for these men, as also for the incoming president, to assert their independence if their former chief is not on the boards with them.

My partners and I hope that you will continue to act as a director of the I.M.M. Company, and also remain a member of the British committee. I hope to have more frequent meetings of the latter and thus to have the benefit of your advice on all general questions of policy. In our conversation in January last you expressed yourself as willing to remain on this committee and I hope that you will not change your decision.

Yours sincerely,

E.C. Grenfell.

Soon after receiving Grenfell's letter, Bruce sent his reply, expressing his disappointment that he would not be required to continue on the boards of the operating companies, especially that of the White Star Line:

October 28th, 1912.

Many thanks for your private and confidential letter of the 23rd inst. contents of which have been read with some measure of disappointment, as I had hoped after what I said to you, that our friends would have been willing that I should continue a director of the White Star Line at any rate; I really do not care one iota about the other companies, but you will appreciate I am bound to have a good deal of sentiment in connection with the White Star Line.

I quite understand junior men will be promoted when I go and rightly so, but I cannot see how my remaining a director of the White Star Line will in any way hamper matters. At present there are only three directors, therefore: four vacancies on the board; why not fill them up and so promote some of the juniors? I cannot think my being on the board would in any way interfere with the incoming president, but if it would do so this ends the matter.

I wish you would reconsider the matter, only so far as the White Star Line is concerned.

It is good of you and your partners wishing me to remain a director of the I.M.M. Company and also a member of the British committee. Perhaps you will kindly let my decision remain in abeyance for a little time, as I want to carefully consider the matter.

I do not propose making any announcement before the end of December, unless anything unforeseen arises.

Almost one month later, Grenfell sent another letter in reply to Ismay. This time the letter was short and much more direct:

22, Old Broad Street,
London, November 21st, 1912.
PRIVATE & CONFIDENTIAL

My dear Ismay,
I was absent yesterday when your letter of the 18th arrived.
Since receiving yours of the 28th ulto, I have had a further discussion with Mr. J.P. Morgan, Junior, on the question of your retaining your directorships of the constituent companies of the I.M.M. Company, after your retirement from the presidency. I fully appreciate your desire from sentiment to remain on the board of the O.S.N. Company, and I much

regret that, after further consideration, I do not see my way to alter the opinion expressed to you in my letter of the 23rd October.

I understand you wish to let your decision as regards the directorship of the I.M.M. Company, remain over until the end of next month.

Yours sincerely,

[signed] E.C. Grenfell.

Another letter arrived, a week later, this time from Harold Sanderson, in which Sanderson supported the views laid down by Grenfell:

My dear Bruce,

I dined with Grenfell last evening, and had the desired opportunity for discussing with him the directorship matter of which he spoke last Wednesday. The result has convinced me that I was correct in concluding that the decision they have reached is to be attributed to a considered and settled policy, and not to any personal feeling towards yourself.

I gathered the impression from Grenfell's remarks that they would not be disposed to depart from the line that has been suggested, and I hope upon reflection, you will agree with the view I expressed to you, i.e., that, as retiring President, your name might very properly be expected to appear amongst the directors of the controlling company (I.M.M. Co.), and that this expectation could hardly apply in the case of any of the boards of the subsidiary companies, not even excepting the O.S.N. Co.

A shocking wet day here.

Yours sincerely,

Harold A. Sanderson.

The following day, Bruce sent a telegram to Grenfell confirming that he would, after his presidency ended, conform to the wish of IMM Co. and remain a director and member of the British Committee. Thus, on 30 June 1913, Bruce Ismay retired from the presidency of IMM, and therefore from the chairmanship of the White Star Line, and by doing so, he lost control of the company that his father had saved from near bankruptcy some forty-five years earlier.

11

LIFE IN IRELAND

Once the British inquiry into the *Titanic* disaster was over, Bruce, along with his wife Florence, began to look for suitable accommodation in which to spend their summer months. They were currently living in a large Georgian house in Mayfair, London, which provided the perfect residence while he was president of IMM, but Bruce now wished to spend more time pursuing his favourite sport, fishing, so the couple journeyed to the Scottish home of his brother, Charles Bower Ismay.

Bower and his wife Constance now had a large country house at Dalnaspidal, Perthshire, Scotland, which was located close to Loch Garry. This provided the ideal location for Bruce to take some solitude while being able to spend much of his time fishing for salmon. It also provided a wonderful opportunity for Florence to spend some time with her younger sister, Constance.

While staying with his brother, Bruce was told of a lodge that had recently come up for sale. The lodge was located in Costelloe, County Galway, Ireland, an area which was noted for having some of the finest fishing grounds in Ireland. The thought of owning the lodge appealed greatly to Bruce, and consequently, he hurriedly purchased the property without viewing it.

It was not until his presidential retirement from IMM in 1913 that he saw the property for the first time. On arrival, Mr and Mrs Ismay were surprised by the lack of services within the lodge. They were already aware that there was no electricity within the property but were surprised to learn that the only water supply was from a nearby well.

The attraction for Bruce was the River Cashla, flowing past the property, with several loughs only a short distance away, providing an excellent opportunity for salmon fishing. Beyond the River Cashla was a large bay, opening up to the North Atlantic Ocean, which was also perfect for sea trout.

Florence insisted that if they were to spend time there, improvements would have to be made to the property. On their return to London, Bruce arranged for major improvement work to be carried out during the winter, stipulating that the work should be completed ready for their return the following summer. Following the renovation work, the couple continued to share their time between Costelloe during the summer, and their London home during the remainder of the year.

After his retirement from presidency of IMM, Bruce was able to greatly reduce his workload and his commitment to the company, thereby giving him more time to pursue his other business interests, including the Liverpool & London Insurance Company, the Globe Insurance Company and the Thames & Mersey Insurance Company, to name just three.

Railways had always been part of Bruce's life, and he always regretted having to step back from this work in order that he could take up his presidency with IMM. He was therefore delighted when he received a letter in late November 1922 informing him that he had been selected to serve on the board of a newly formed railway company, to be known as the London Midland & Scottish Railway. He happily accepted this directorship, and it was proposed that Mr Ismay should serve on the committees for traffic, rolling stock, shipping and stores.

On several occasions, the board of directors asked Bruce to accept chairmanship of the London Midland & Scottish Railway, but he always declined. However, he did agree to take chairmanship of the company's finance committee. His memories of the *Titanic* disaster, especially those associated with the press, ensured that he would never again be willing to stand so prominently within the view of the public eye.

In the same year, Mr and Mrs Ismay received news that their Costelloe home had been burned to the ground during the Irish Civil War. Both Bruce and Florence were devastated to hear the news, but it provided them with the opportunity to completely rebuild their summer home. In 1925, work began on the new Costelloe Lodge. The replacement was to be much larger than the original, with many design ideas coming from Florence. The couple were delighted with their new home, which was now preferable to their Mayfair residence, but as most of Bruce's work was located in London, they continued to live in Mayfair during the winter months, and additionally when their family interests required their presence in London.

Life in Costelloe was much more tranquil than their lifestyle in London. Nevertheless, Bruce and Florence employed a large number of people to help look after the estate and associated fishing grounds. To help prevent poaching, several water bailiffs were employed, while two gardeners kept the grounds in good order. The house staff, which generally included the butlers, maids and cooks who were usually employed at their Hill Street residence in Mayfair, travelled to Costelloe in advance, so that all would be ready for Bruce and Florence's arrival, the exception being Bruce's personal butler and close friend, Mr John Smith, who often travelled with them.

Although the Costelloe residence was primarily intended for the summer months, Bruce and Florence would occasionally spend time there during winter, with Christmas being a favourite. 'There used to be a huge hooley once a year in the house. There was food and drink and plenty of both.'[1] After such occasions, Mr and Mrs Ismay would send food packages to children attending the local school.

Bruce and Florence loved the local community, and they were liked and respected within the village. According to one newspaper report, 'People spoke highly of them for the simple reason they gave a lot of employment to the area. This area was very poor then. People were just eking out a living out of fishing and small farms.'[2]

Florence Ismay cared deeply about the local children, often visiting the local school. 'Mrs Ismay used to visit the national school every year at the end of September or the beginning of October. It was at the end of the fishing season and before she went back to London.'[3] During these school visits, Florence would enter every classroom, leaving a box of sweets in each one, with one student later saying, 'They were the first sweets we ever saw with wrapping on them.'[4]

While at Costelloe, Bruce employed Mr Coleman, a local carpenter, to undertake general maintenance within the lodge and grounds. Mr Coleman had a son who wished to apply for entry into the naval college, and he asked Bruce to write a letter of reference on his behalf. Bruce Ismay replied, 'If your son will give my name to the naval people in Liverpool I will be glad to answer any questions they put, that I am able to do. Will help in any way I can. Yours truly, Bruce Ismay.'[5]

Mr and Mrs Ismay spent many happy years living between Costelloe and London, with Bruce's business interests keeping him busy throughout his later years. However, at 70 years of age, just seven years after the rebuilding of the lodge, Bruce's health began to fail, and it was now time for him to withdraw from his various directorships. He was suffering from severe pains in his legs, which began to affect his mobility.

Eventually, Bruce's failing health necessitated him to become dependent on others to help him throughout the day. Consequently, he asked Mr John Smith, who had been his butler and close friend and had retired some twelve months earlier, to return to Costelloe to oversee the packing, as the lodge was to remain unoccupied throughout the winter, with Mr and Mrs Ismay returning to their Hill Street residence.

During the winter, Bruce underwent an operation to have the lower part of his right leg amputated. John Smith took great care of him throughout his recovery and rarely left his side. Bruce was now dependant on a wheelchair and crutches to help him get around. He quickly realised that he would never again visit Costelloe Lodge and the fishing grounds he had loved so much.

Throughout the following three years of his life, Bruce made every effort to preserve his independence by employing mechanical aids to assist his everyday personal needs. Naturally, he realised that his health would never improve but remained thankful that the surgeon was able to save the upper part of his right leg.

In the autumn of 1934, Mr and Mrs Ismay, along with their butler, travelled to Farnborough for a short break, returning to their London home in October. On the evening of the 14th, their butler had prepared a bath for Bruce. When he later returned to the bedroom, he was shocked to find Bruce unconscious in an armchair aside the bed. With assistance, he managed to move him onto his bed.

Bruce had suffered a massive stroke, which had taken his sight and his speech. He remained there for three days, during which time his wife never left his side. Bruce died soon after midday on 17 October 1937, without ever regaining full consciousness.

On the following Monday morning, two days after Bruce Ismay's death, Mr Frank Bustard, the last apprentice to serve under Bruce and who eventually became passenger traffic manager for the White Star Line, unlocked his London office. He was horrified to find that a mirror, which Bruce had given him upon completion of his apprenticeship many years earlier, lay shattered on the office floor.

Appendix 1

Extracts from the Archives

Extract from Uldale Parish Register, 1754:

Daniel Ismay of the Parish of Bromfield & County of Cumberland and Ann Cowx of this Parish, were married in this Church by License this twelfth Day of November, One Thousand seven Hundred & Fifty Four By me Barzillai Rowland Curate.

This marriage was solemnized between us Daniel Ismay, Ann Cowx X her mark. In the presence of John Cowx, Joseph Pape.'[1]

Extract from Uldale Parish Register, 1777:

Thomas Ismay, Carpenter, aged 22 and Elizabeth Scott, Spinster aged 22 both of this parish were married in this church by Banns this 27 Day of July in the year 1777. By me Richard Moore, Curate. This marriage was solemnized between us Thomas Ismay Elizabeth Ismay late Scott X her mark in the presence of Joseph Cape and Thomas Wilson.[2]

Extract from Maryport Parish Register, 1800:

Henry Ismay of this parish Bachelor and Mariner and Charlotte Middleton of this parish, Spinster were married in this church by License this twenty eight day of January in the Year One thousand eight hundred. By me Wm Passable Curate. This marriage was solemnized between us Henry Ismay, Charlotte Middleton in the presence of Richard Wallas and Martha Smith.[3]

Extract from Maryport Parish Register, 1836:

Joseph Ismay of this parish, Bachelor and Shipwright and Mary Sealby of this parish, Spinster were married in this church by License this Seventh day of April in the Year One thousand eight hundred and thirty six. By me John Donald, Curate. This marriage was solemnized between us Joseph Ismay, Mary Sealby in the presence of Robert Thompson, Betsey Millican.[4]

Extract from Maryport Parish Register, 1837:

Church of England, Parish Registers – Maryport, Cumberland, England, baptism:
2 February 1837, Thomas Henry son of Joseph & Mary Ismay of Maryport, Shipwright.[5]

The will of Thomas Ismay (born in 1800, Thomas was the son of Henry Ismay and uncle of Thomas Henry Ismay [White Star Line]. He was lost at sea in 1830):

> I Thomas Ismay do hereby give and bequeath to Mr. Joseph Ismay of Maryport the son of Henry Ismay the sum of eighty pounds sterling. Also to Henry Ismay son of the above Henry Ismay all my nautical instruments and watch, or if they be lost or destroyed before he receive them, the sum of forty pounds in lieu of them. Also to Charlotte Clark daughter of the above Henry Ismay the sum of forty pounds sterling. The remainder of my property of every description I bequeath to Charlotte Ismay wife of the above Henry Ismay of Maryport to her sole use and benefit for the sake of bringing up and educating the younger children. I also appoint the above Joseph Ismay of Maryport sole executor to see the above purposes duly fulfilled. I also declare this to be my last will and testament and revoke and annul any formerly made as witness my hand Thomas Ismay. Witnesses John Dixon, Richard Parry and Wm. Middleton. November 21, 1829.[6]

An extract from an insurance policy in respect of *Vine*, mastered by Thomas Ismay and built by Middleton's shipbuilders, Maryport:

London, 26th January 1819

To Sanderson Bros., Dr

For the cost of insurance in the following terms – viz. In the name of God Amen. Sanderson Brothers as agents, as well in their own name, as for and in the name and names of all and every other person or persons to whom the same doth, may, or shall appertain, in part or in all, doth make assurance and cause themselves and them and every of them, to be insured, last or not lost.

At and from the eighteenth day of January 1819 to the seventh day of April 1819 both inclusive – Maryport and at sea in the Coal and Coasting trade of the United Kingdom.

Upon any kind of goods and merchandizes, and also upon the Body, Tackle, Apparel, Ordinance, Munition, artillery, Boat, and other furniture of and in the good Ship or Vessel called the '*Vine*' where of is Master, under God, for this present voyage 'Henry Ismay'

The agreement between the Assureds and Assurers in this policy, are and shall be valued at £150 on ship for interest and an account of Mr. Henry Ismay at and after the rate of Four Guineas per cent.[7]

The Times, Wednesday, 10 April 1907:

MRS. ISMAY, widow of Mr. Thomas Henry Ismay, the founder of the White Star Line, and mother of Mr. Bruce Ismay, head of the International Mercantile Marine Company, died yesterday morning, at the residence of her daughter, Mrs. Geoffrey Drage, in Cadogan-square, London, where she had been staying for some months. Mrs. Ismay had been in failing health for some time. She was the daughter of the late Mr. Luke Bruce, shipowner, and was married, in 1859, to Mr. Ismay, by whom she had a family of three sons and four daughters. Since her husband's death in November, 1899, Mrs. Ismay had lived in retirement at Dawpool, Thurstaston, Cheshire. In the early part of 1900, in accordance with her husband's wish, she gave £10,000 to establish the Margaret Ismay Widows' Fund as a continuation of the Liverpool Seamen's Pension Fund, founded by her husband, under the Mercantile

Marine Service Association, in 1887, by a gift of £20,000. Mrs. Ismay augmented her gift in October last by a further donation of £5,000. She also contributed £10,000 to the Liverpool Cathedral scheme, and had agreed to provide the great east window of the Cathedral in memory of her husband, while she augmented the benefice of Thurstaston, and the new Dawpool schools were almost entirely the result of her generosity. She was in her 70th year. The funeral will take place at Thurstaston Church, at 3 30 on Friday afternoon.[8]

The Cecil Hotel,
Western Parade,
Southsea
July 31st

To Bruce Ismay Esq

Dear Sir,

I feel that I cannot let the finding of the court re loss of *Titanic* pass without conveying to you my delight at Lord Mersey's decision in reference to you for you have indeed had my sympathy throughout & I felt that all you did was perfectly just & right. This inquiry was perfectly just & right. This inquiry must have been a most trying time for you & I am thankful to see that it has come to an end. I am living in a boarding house here with about 40 others, and you have had the sympathy of nearly all.

Yours Sincerely,

T. Lee

Mother of a wireless operator.[9]

After the British inquiry was over, Bruce travelled to his brother's home in Scotland. While staying there, he received a letter from his son, Tom:

Sandheys,
Mossley Hill,
Liverpool

Dearest father,

This is just a line to let you know how sorry I am that I did not see more of you today, and to tell you that I quite realise what an ordeal you had to go through and how deeply I feel for you, however I very much hope the worst is over now and that you will never again be misjudged and your words be misinterpreted as they have been in the present inquiry. I hope you will be benefited by your stay at Dalnaspidal and not be worried by any anonymous communications. I hope you will have fine weather and be able to get some fishing. Evelyn and I went to the cricket ground this afternoon. It rained a good deal, though some of the games were very close being mostly finals. I hope you did not meet much rain on your run up to Carlisle, and that you will not be recognised as I know how you must hate to be before the public eye especially under the present trying circumstances.

I know this letter is very badly expressed, but I hope, you will realise that the spirit in which it is written is none the less sincere for that.

With hopes that your stay in Scotland will be a complete rest I will close.

I am always your loving son,
Tom.[10]

'Man in the Street' extract (newspaper and exact date unknown):

There is no ground for the suggestion that any other life would have been saved if Mr. Ismay had not got into the boat' he said. 'The boat was actually being lowered, and if Mr. Ismay had not gone in it, the only result would have been that the boat would have left with that space empty.'

Taking the war into the enemy's camp, Sir Robert added, 'If Mr. Ismay had committed suicide in that way, his present critics would have said he did so because he dared not face the inquiry into the loss of the vessel.'

MARYPORT-BUILT SAILING SHIPS OF THE NINETEENTH CENTURY

Clytie (1824)

Clytie was a brig built at Maryport by Isaac Middleton and launched on 23 September 1824. In 1840, she was registered at Maryport, owned by Captain John Jackson (her master) and others.

Countess of Liverpool (1824)

Countess of Liverpool was built at Maryport by Isaac Middleton and launched on 8 October 1824. The following is a letter from Mr Lindsay of Liverpool, one of the passengers on board the brig. He describes an encounter with a pirate ship:

> Buenos Ayres, December 20 – We arrived here on the 15th instant, after a long and rough passage of 79 days. On

the 12th November, at daylight, we saw a sail to wind-
ward, steering towards us. At half-past nine a.m., she came
within musket shot, when she fired a gun from her starboard side across our stern, hoisted Buenos Ayres colours,
beat to quarters, and lowered four boats, with about thirty
armed men.

The first person that came on board of us was the officer
in command. He was a little man, of dark complexion, wore
a high-crowned hat, and had a brace of pistols in his belt,
(on the barrels of which were the letters D.C.L.) and a
cutlass in his hand. His men were armed with a brace of pistols, a knife, and a cutlass. On coming on board, they asked
Captain Jenkinson the name of his vessel, where from, and
whither bound, our latitude and longitude, and if we had
seen many ships on our passage. After Captain Jenkinson
had answered these questions, the officer of the pirate told
us he had been cruising off Cadiz, that he was short of
provisions, and that if we would supply him with some, he
would give us a bill for the amount upon a house in Buenos
Ayres. To this proposal, Captain Jenkinson readily agreed.
The villain now began to show himself in his true colours.
He asked Captain Jenkinson for his cabin boy. The captain
having told him he had none, the officer of the pirate immediately struck the captain across the back a number of times
with his cutlass in the most brutal manner. He then ordered
the provisions and ship stores to be brought up on deck,
which having been done; he helped himself to whatever he
pleased. After sending his boats to the pirate vessel, loaded
with provisions, &c., he proceeded to rifle the cargo. Silk
handkerchiefs and stockings were thrown about the deck
in all directions, as also a great many barrels of ale. They
[the pirates] took a box of coats belonging to Mr. Claypole,
Whitechapel, valued at £100.

What quantity of goods they took altogether is not known, as they would not allow the captain to take either the number or marks of anything. After robbing us of nearly all our provisions and part of the cargo, they began with the passengers. The officer of the pirate ordered me to follow him down to the cabin, where I had to turn out the contents of my trunks, from which he took, in cloth and clothes, to the value of £30. Previous to this pirate coming alongside of us, Captain Jenkinson gave me a gold watch, a case of watches directed to Hess, and four small parcels, directed to Helsby, all of which I put under my bed. After rummaging my trunks, the officer of the pirate proceeded to search under the bed, and, having found the watch, quickly put it in his pocket. Some musical snuff-boxes, directed to Helsby, he would not have, and the case of watches, directed to Hess, he did not find. From Mr. Hardacre, a passenger, the pirates took a handsome gold watch, and nearly the whole of his boots, shoes, and shirts; from Mr. Symes, a dentist, another passenger, four dozen of shirts, all his boots and shoes, many of his tools, and about 280 dollars, and afterwards beat him with their cutlasses in a shocking manner. They took the whole of the cabin stores, and only left the captain the shirt he had on his back.

As they were about to leave us, the officer ordered Mrs. Lindsay and myself to follow him into the cabin. On getting below, he politely handed Mrs. L. to a chair, and the next moment he placed a pistol to my head, threatening to blow my brains out if I did not give him all the money I had got. I told him that I and everyone else in the ship was at his mercy, as we were all unarmed, and, therefore, he might do as he chose, but that money I had none. Mrs. L. offered him two sovereigns, but he was too gallant to take the money from her. The pirates left us about two o'clock in the afternoon, and steered away North West.

Eliza (1835)

Eliza was a snow, built by Isaac Middleton at Maryport and launched on 21 December 1835. She was registered at Whitehaven initially, then at Lancaster from 1839.

Grace (1816)

Grace was a brig, built at Maryport by Isaac Middleton in 1816:

> The *Grace*, Darling, of this port, was abandoned on the 12th ult., in lat. 39° 26' N, long. 39° 50' W. Sailed from Manzanillo on the 1st of October. After a succession of contrary winds, passed Cape Floriday on the 6th of November. Had nothing but heavy weather, with strong gales, and ship labouring and making water. When running in a gale of wind from N.W. a sea struck the ship with great violence on the port quarter, and carried away the rudder stock close to the dead wood. The captain writes that after using every effort to secure the rudder, but without avail, the ship being then quite unmanageable, bulwarks washed away, and other damage, they had prepared the long boat to leave the ship, when a Danish schooner hove in sight and took the crew aboard. They were landed at Deal on the 30th ult., all well.[1]

Henry Ismay (1845)

Henry Ismay was launched in Maryport on 3 November 1845, a brigantine of 147 tonnes owned by Joseph Ismay, father of Thomas Henry Ismay.

Mary Ismay (1849)

Mary Ismay was built at Middleton's shipbuilding yard and launched in 1849. The ship was a brig of 162 tonnes and was launched fully sailed, immediately making her maiden voyage around Cape Horn.

Middleton (1839)

Middleton was built at Middleton's shipyard and was a brig of 241 tonnes. She was intended for service on the West Indies and South American trade routes.

Vine (1812)

Built in Maryport, *Vine* was a schooner of 86 tonnes:

> Captained by Henry Ismay, with a crew of five the *Vine* arrived at St. John's, Newfoundland in May 1813, having departed from Liverpool and having joined a convoy at Cork. The schooner returned to Liverpool, arriving on the 9th August. She then repeated the voyage, departing Cork as part of a convoy on the 3rd October and arriving in Newfoundland in December.[2]

WHITE STAR LINE HANDBOOK

The following is a copy of the White Star Line Rules and Regulations Handbook, given to officers and commanders when sailing the Liverpool to New York passage:

WHITE STAR LINE–OCEANIC STEAM NAVIGATION COMPANY, LTD.
Regulations for the Safe and Efficient Navigation of the Company's Steamships.

GENERAL RULES.
1. *Instructions to be attended to.* The Company's commanders and officers are particularly enjoined to make themselves not only acquainted, but familiar with the following rules and regulations.
2. *Responsibility of Commanders.* The commanders must distinctly understand that the issue of the following instructions does not in any way relieve them from entire responsibility for the safe and efficient navigation of their respective vessels; and they are also enjoined to remem-

ber that, whilst they are expected to use every diligence to secure a speedy voyage, they must run no risk which might by any possibility result in accident to their ships. It is to be hoped that they will ever bear in mind that the safety of lives and property entrusted to their care is the ruling principles that should govern them in the navigation of their ships and no supposed gain in expedition, or saving of time on the voyage, is to be purchased at the risk of accident. The Company desires to establish and maintain for its vessels a reputation for safety, and only looks for such speed on various voyages as is consistent with safe and prudent navigation.

3. *Authority of Commanders.* The officers, engineers, and all others borne upon the ship's books, are subject to the control and orders of the commander, and all on board, of every rank, must be careful to respect his authority. Leave of absence in all cases, is only to be granted by the commander or commanding officer for the time being, and the return to duty must be reported in a like manner; it being understood that in no case, when the ship is in a foreign port, are the chief and second officers to be absent from the ship at the same time, and that a junior officer is always to be on board.

4. *Respect due to officers.* Every superior officer is to exact, upon all occasions, from those under him, unequivocal and respectful compliance with his orders, and it is expected of all that they will not neglect the usual exterior mark of respect, either when they address or are addressed by a superior officer.

5. *Watches.* The watches must be equally divided, and the ship is never to be left without an officer in charge of the deck, either at sea or in harbour; and no officer is, on any occasion, to leave the deck during his watch, nor

until he is relieved of his duty; and officers are expected, when performing the duties of the ship, or when at their different stations, to preserve silence among the men, and to see that orders from the bridge or upper deck are executed with promptitude, and without confusion or noise. At sea, when the officer of the watch believes his ship to be running into danger, it is his duty to act, at once, upon his own responsibility; at the same time, he must pass the word to call the commander. The first and second officers should never give up charge of the bridge during their watch excepting in clear weather and open sea, when they may be relieved for their meals by the third and fourth officers, but at no other time, unless with the express permission of the commander.

6. *Watch in dock, Liverpool.* In dock, at Liverpool, an officer is always to be on deck with the quartermaster as a day watch, until relieved by the night officer, one quartermaster and one watchman.

7. *Watch in dock, abroad.* In port abroad, an officer of the ship is always to be on the upper or spar deck, in charge, together with the two quartermasters in the day-time. At night the watch is to be kept by an officer and two quartermasters.

8. *Anchor watch.* In harbour, when the ship is at anchor, the watch, night and day, is to consist of a junior officer, two quartermasters and four seamen.

9. *Junior officers.* The junior officers must exert themselves to afford every assistance in the navigation of the ship, by perfecting themselves in the practice of solar and stellar observations, both for the correction of the compasses and ascertaining the position of the ship.

10. *Junior officers.* In ships carrying third and fourth officers, those officers are not to have charge of a watch at sea except at the discretion of the commander.

11. *Log and observations for position of ship.* The log to be regularly hove, and the ship's position to be ascertained each day by solar observation when obtainable. The chief officer is required to work up the ship's position as soon after noon as practicable, and then to take it to the commander in the chart-room, where he will see the place of the ship pricked on the chart, so as always to keep himself posted as to steamer's position and course.

12. *Compasses.* The compasses should be carefully watched, and any difference that may be observed between the local deviation and that shown by the table of corrections to be noted in the compass-book kept for the purpose.

13. *Night order book.* The commander to enter in the night order book the course to be steered, and all other necessary instructions.

14. *Nearing the land and heaving the lead.* A wide berth to be given to all headlands, islands, shoals, and the coast generally; and the commanders are particularly enjoined, on all occasions when nearing the land or in places of intricate navigation, to take frequent cross-bearings of any well-marked objects that may be visible and suitable for verifying the position of the ship. Should the weather be unsuitable for cross-bearings the engines should be eased, and, if necessary, stopped occasionally, and casts of the deep sea lead taken.

    The steam-whistle to be sounded during the prevalence of fogs, and the fact recorded in the log book.

15. *Boats, fire-hose, pumps etc.* A crew to be appointed to each boat, which, with the tackling, is required to be kept in good order and ready for immediate service. The ship's company to be exercised at their stations occasionally, in working the pumps, fire-hose, and handing along buckets, etc., so that the crew may be kept in proper

training and the stores in efficient order, in case of fire or other accident.

16. *Lights.* The side and mast-head lights to be particularly attended to and always ready, and when in use to be placed according to Government regulations. All lights, except such as the captain or executive officer shall suffer (or the law requires), are to be put out every evening at 10 o'clock in forecastle and steerage, at 11 o'clock in the saloon, at 11.15 p.m. in the smoke rooms, and at 11.30 o'clock in the sleeping berths or state rooms.

17. *Fires.* No fire to be allowed in the galleys after 10 o'clock p. m., unless with the express permission of the commander.

18. *Sounding the wells, etc.* The holds and fresh water tanks to be sounded twice a day by the carpenter, who is also required to turn the cocks in the water-tight bulkheads every 24 hours; pump gear to be examined, and everything kept in order for immediate use. A sounding book must be kept by the carpenter, and each examination recorded. The chief officer to inspect the book daily and initial it.

19. *Inspection of ship by commander.* The commander is expected to make a thorough inspection of the ship, at least once in every 24 hours, accompanied by the purser and surgeon. 11 a.m. would probably be found the most convenient hour for this duty. In the engine room inspection, the commander should be attended by the chief engineer only.

20. *Spirit-room.* The spirit-room is, under no circumstances, to be opened except during the day, and then only in the presence of the purser. No light is to be taken into the spirit-room on any pretext whatever. The key of the spirit-room to be kept by the purser.

21. *Smoking.* Smoking by the officers when on duty is strictly prohibited, and is allowed only in their own cabins or on the main deck, but on no account in any of the companion ways. Smoking by seamen, firemen, stewards, and others, allowed only on the main deck, forward of the main mast, when off duty.

22. *Parcels; etc.*, not to be carried by ship's company. No parcels or goods of any description are to be carried by the ship's company for any person whatsoever.

23. *Smuggling.* The ship is to be searched for contraband goods before entering any port, and the result entered in the official log book. The chief of each department to conduct the search, accompanied by the purser. Any person detected smuggling will be dismissed from service, any fines incurred being deducted from the wages due to the offender; and the heads of the different departments will be held responsible for those people immediately under their orders.

24. *Signal lights.* Rockets and blue or green lights, especially company's private signals, to be always kept at hand, ready for night signals, but on no account to be stowed in the powder magazine.

25. *Flags.* In port, from the 21st day of March to the 21st day of September, the ensign and company's signal to be hoisted at 8.30 a.m., and from the 22nd day of September to the 20th day of March, at 9 a.m., and hauled down at sunset. In stormy weather, small flags must be substituted.

26. *Punishment.* No man to be confined or punished in any-way, when the commander is on board, without his order, and the punishment must be registered in the official log book. In the absence of the captain, the offender is to be confined, if it be necessary, but at no time in port, without acquainting the peace authorities

of the port; if at a wharf, or in dock, the police are to be called promptly.

27. *Uniform.* The uniform prescribed by the company is to be worn on board, at all times, by the officers (the engineer on watch excepted). The crew (consisting of the seamen, firemen, and stewards), excepting firemen on duty, must always wear it on Sundays, at sea or in port; also on the days of sailing from or arriving in port, each one of the crew being compelled to provide himself with a uniform.

28. *Divine Service.* Divine service is to be performed on board every Sunday, weather permitting.

29. *Report on officers.* The commanders are required to give a faithful and conscientious report of the conduct, qualifications, and sobriety of officers, engineers, and petty officers, individually, at the end of each voyage.

30. *Rules of the road.* The commanders and officers of the several ships are strictly enjoined to make themselves perfectly familiar with the rules of the road, as issued by the Board of Trade, a copy being attached hereto for general reference.

31. *Change of commanders.* When any change of commander takes place, the officer relieved must hand to his successor this Book of Instructions, the copy of mail contract (if any), and all other ship's papers, especially those relating to the compasses and chronometers.

32. *Log-Book.* The log-book is to be kept by the chief officer, who is required to write it up daily from the log-slate, and submit it for the commander's inspection and signature.

33. *Log-slate; directions for keeping it.* The log-slate to be carefully written up, by the officer in charge of the deck, every watch, at sea or in port, and the particulars noted below punctually attended to:-

(i) Courses (in degrees) by standard compass.

(ii) Courses (in degrees) true.

(iii) Speed of ship by log.

(iv) Direction and force of wind.

(v) Barometer and thermometer.

(vi) Revolutions of engines.

(vii) Number of inches of water in the wells.

(viii) Remarks upon the weather, and other particulars; such as, what sail set and when taken in, if any and what signals are made, vessels met or spoken, especially those belonging to the company.

(iv) The true bearings and distance of any land or lights in sight, particularly cross-bearings.

(x) When and what soundings are obtained.

(xi) Lunar or stellar observations, azimuths, or amplitudes.

(xii) Time of arrival and departure from any place, with the ship's draught of water.

(xiii) Time when passengers (and mails, if any) are landed and embarked.

(xiv) Any births or deaths that may occur on board and in the latter case time of burial.

(xv) When and for what purpose boats leave the ship and return.

(xvi) When the anchor is let go at any port or place, the depth of water, the number of fathoms of cable veered to, and cross bearings taken to determine the exact position of the ship.

(xvii) How the hands of watches arc employed during the day.

(xviii) The exact quantity of coal and water received at the respective ports, and the expenditure each day.

(xix) Any case of collision or touching the ground, or other accident, to be carefully noted, giving the name of the officer of the watch, and the names and stations of the men on the lookout.

(xx) Any case of misconduct among the crew (required by the Merchant Seamen's Act), particularly in reference to forfeiture of wages.

(xxi) When the ship's company are exercised at their stations.

(xxii) When Divine service is performed, or why omitted.

(xxiii) The names of all persons on the sick list to be entered each day at noon.

(xxiv) The ship's reckoning, up to noon each day, both by observation and account, complete.

34. *Log-book.* The log, when completed by the chief officer, is to have its correctness certified by the officer of each watch, and to be placed before the commander daily for his inspection and signature.

35. *Log-book.* A leaf must never be removed or closed up in the log-book, nor an erasure made under any circumstances, but all errors are to be cancelled by ruling a line through them, with the initials attached.

36. *Log-book.* At the end of the voyage the log-book must be signed by the commander and chief officer, and then delivered over to the managers of the company.

37. *Engineer's log-book to be examined by the commander.* The commander is required each day to examine and sign the engineer's log-book, and shall be responsible for any omission that may occur in the same. The commander is likewise enjoined to pay special attention to the daily consumption and remaining stock of coal.

38. *Tracks.* It is not desirable to specify in these instructions any particular route to take between Liverpool and New York, as commanders must, in a great measure, be left to their own judgment in the matter, and be guided by

circumstances; but the following may be taken as a guide, as emanating from officers of great experience in the Atlantic trade:-

'We consider the best and safest track to take in crossing the Banks of Newfoundland, say, from the middle of March to the middle of December, is to strike the Flemish Cap, and then shape a course to take the ship about 35 miles south of Virgin Rocks. The remaining three months we think it prudent to take the southern passage, as the field-ice is then forming on the edge of the banks'.

Note:- During the month of November and half of December, the passage via Cape Race may be taken with safety, there being little fog there at the time.

Sable Island. This island should always be passed to the westward, as strong currents, fogs, and great local attraction are known to exist in the channel, between the island and the main, rendering the navigation extremely hazardous.

Skerries. The commanders are required invariably to pass to the northward, or outside this group of rocks, the channel inside being considered too narrow and dangerous to admit of large steamers being navigated through in perfect safety.

Course down channel. In leaving Liverpool, after passing the Skerries, it is usual in all steam-ship lines to steer for the Stack; with the Stack abeam and close aboard, shape a course for the Saltees Lightship; this will take a steamer about four miles south of the fair way of steam-ships, and ships, with a fair wind, bound to Liverpool.

39. *Special reports.* Commanders are required to furnish the managers with a special report, in writing, of any unusual occurrence which may have taken place on board, or in

connection with their ships – such as accidents to life or limb, misconduct or mismanagement on the part of, or any serious complaint against, any of the company's servants, or anything requiring an entry in the official log of the vessel.

40. This book is to be returned to the company's office in the event of the holder leaving the service.

STEAMERS' NIGHT SIGNALS

WHITE STAR LINE–Green light, rocket throwing two green stars, and green light in succession.

ACKNOWLEDGEMENTS

I am extremely grateful to the Cheape family for allowing me access to their extensive family archive, including letters, photographs and diaries. I am also grateful for the hospitality extended to me during my visit and for the subsequent conversations we had, without all of which this book would not have been possible. Unless otherwise stated, letters and diary entries in this book are by courtesy of the Cheape family.

A special thanks to Tad Fitch, who kindly wrote the fore-word for this book and quickly provided a lifeboat or two when needed, I will be forever grateful.

I would like to thank Mr George Behe, former vice president of the Titanic Historical Society and notable author of many books, for introducing me to The History Press, and for the many *Titanic* communications we have had. Further thanks to George for kindly giving me permission to reproduce transcriptions from the Titanic Inquiry Project, and for his help and guidance throughout.

I was fortunate to have had several correspondences with Ann Marie Nielsen, who has given me an interesting insight into the life of her relative, Australian *Titanic* survivor, Evelyn Marsden.

My gratitude is also extended to Amy Rigg, commissioning editor with The History Press, whose advice and guidance has proved invaluable. Thanks are also due to my editor Jezz Palmer, as well as the board members of The History Press for considering the publication of yet another *Titanic*-related book.

A huge thank you to Rosita Boland and *The Irish Times* for adding further insight into Bruce and Florence's later years spent in and around Costelloe, Ireland.

I am also grateful to Mr Anthony Frazer for supplying me with an image of his family portrait of Thomas Henry Ismay, painted by Sir Hubert Herkomer, and to Beken Archives for permission to use their photograph of *Olympic* at sea.

My gratitude and thanks to many notable *Titanic* and White Star Line historians, namely: Helen Benziger, for her contributions; William Brower, for helping to keep me on the straight and narrow while researching *Titanic*; Mark Chirnside, for his advice in helping clear up some conflicting opinions; Dave Gardner, for his valuable insight into late nineteenth-century New York; Tom Lynskey, for sharing his detailed knowledge of *Titanic*; Jonathon Wild, who has extensive knowledge of Liverpool throughout the nineteenth century, particularly the White Star Line; and Bill Willard, for his contribution to this book.

Special thanks are also due to author Bruce Beveridge for permission to use his wonderful and highly accurate plan of *Titanic*'s Boat Deck, and to J. Kent Layton for sharing images of *Titanic* from his collection.

Thank you to Nor Holzt-Gibbons and her father, Tommy Canavan, for their insight into Third Class passenger, Patrick Canavan.

My sincere love and gratitude go to my wife Annette who has tolerated me locking myself in the study with the other lady in my life, RMS *Titanic*. Thanks are also extended to my children for their support, especially my son Callum for his help and inspiration throughout.

Photo Credits

Unless otherwise stated, images in this book are by courtesy of the Cheape family.

Other Sources
White Star Line head office, Liverpool: Jonathon Wild.
White Star Line's first class ticket office, Liverpool: Jonathon Wild.
Titanic Boat Deck technical drawing: Bruce Beveridge.
Titanic at sea image: J. Kent Layton Collection.
Titanic wreck images: RMS *Titanic* Inc., Georgia, USA.
Olympic at sea: courtesy of Beken Archive, Cowes, Isle of Wight.

I apologise if I have unknowingly infringed anyone's copyright. If this is the case, please let me know so that corrections may be made in any future edition.

NOTES

Unless otherwise specified, all sources come from the Cheape Archives.

Chapter 3

1 Wilton J. Oldham, *The Ismay Line*, The Journal of Commerce, Liverpool, 1961
2 *Ibid.*

Chapter 4

1 *The Times*, London, 1899.

Chapter 5

1 'Ismay One Name Study' – http://ismay.one-name.net

Chapter 9

1 Gareth Russell, *The Ship of Dreams*, William Collins, London, 2019
2 George Behe, Titanic Inquiry Project.
3 *Ibid.*

Chapter 11

1 Rosita Boland, *Irish Times*, Dublin 2020.
2 *Ibid.*
3 *Ibid.*
4 *Ibid.*
5 *Ibid.*

Appendix 1

1 'Ismay One Name Study' – http://ismay.one-name.net
2 *Ibid.*
3 *Ibid.*
4 *Ibid.*
5 *Ibid.*
6 *Ibid.*
7 *Ibid.*
8 *The Times*, London, 1907.
9 The Cheape family.
10 *Ibid.*

Appendix 2

1 *Cumberland Pacquet and Ware's Whitehaven Advertiser*, 6 January 1857.
2 *Lloyd's Register of Shipping*, 1813.

BIBLIOGRAPHY

Books

Fitch, Tad; Layton, J. Kent & Wormstedt, Bill, *On A Sea Of Glass*,
Amberley, Gloucestershire, 2015.

Oldham, Wilton J., *The Ismay Line*, Journal of Commerce,
Liverpool, 1961

Ismay Testimonial Book, 1885. (Special edition; no further
information available).

Robinson, Annie, *The White Star Line*, Allerdale District Council,
Allerdale, 1974.

Littlejohn, Philip, Titanic: *'Waiting For Orders'*, The Crescent Company,
Maidenhead, 1999.

Lord, Walter, *A Night To Remember*, Penguin, Middlesex, 1976.

Primary Sources

The Cheape Family Archive, original private letters, business letters and
memorandums used throughout this publication.

The Cheape Family Archive, diary entries from Mrs Margaret
Ismay's diary.

Internet-Based Sources

Grace's Guide to British Industrial History, www.gracesguide.co.uk.
Titanic Inquiry Project, by kind permission of Mr George Behe,
     www.titanicinquiry.org.
Ismay One Name Study, by kind permission of David Nixon,
     ismay.one-name.net.

Newspapers

The Times, London
The Irish Times, Dublin

INDEX

J. Bruce Ismay is abbreviated to JBI.

GENERAL INDEX

SHIPS OF THE WHITE STAR LINE

SHIPS OWNED BY OTHER COMPANIES